THE SIXTIES IN BR

The Sixties
in
Bristol

as recalled by:

Mary Ackland · Ros Anstey · James Belsey
George Ferguson · Jeremy Brien
David Harrison · Helen Reid · A.C.H. Smith

Editor: James Belsey

REDCLIFFE
Bristol

First published in 1989
by Redcliffe Press Ltd.,
49 Park St., Bristol.

© Redcliffe Press Ltd

ISBN 0 948265 34 5

Typeset and printed by
WBC Print Ltd., Bristol and Maesteg

Contents

JAMES BELSEY

Introduction

You'd turn a corner near the City Centre and see the most extraordinary sight, a great grey or white wall which appeared to move before your eyes. Your heart might miss a beat until you realised: it was an ocean-going ship under way, glimpsed between tall quayside buildings.

Or you could wander around Bathurst Basin and buy a pint of cloudy draught cider at the run-down Ostrich Inn with its dilapidated bus seats arranged around the walls. Outside, the derelict wharves were knee deep in ragwort and grasses, rosebay willow herb and buddleia. The undergrowth hid the neglected dockside workings, the engine houses, rusting machinery and dulled railway lines. But dominating the scene were the warehouses, great red brick cathedrals of a lost religion of mercantile endeavour.

In the winter, if the air was still enough and a mist hung over the city, it mingled with the smoke from tens of thousands of coal fires and became a soupy fog, sometimes so thick it was difficult to cross a wide road without losing your bearings. And in the winter, if the wind was gentle and the weather warm, Bedminster and Ashton, Hotwells and the lower Clifton slopes had a nose-wrinkling smell of sewage as the tides did their best to flush away the city's detritis from the River Avon.

There was another tide – the cars. They flowed in each morning from the new commuterlands of North Somerset and South Gloucestershire and they ebbed back to Nailsea and Portishead, Yate and Sodbury in the afternoon. Civil engineers – the 1960s was the heyday of the civil engineer – built wider, bigger roads to hurry them over Cumberland Basin, past Broadmead and into traffic jams which were modest by today's standards but which argued, they said, that Bristol needed more, still bigger highways.

The civil engineers and architects joined forces to send a new generation of buildings soaring upwards and sideways: city centre office blocks to hide Bristol's centuries old skyline of towers and spires, urban and suburban high-rise blocks of council flats to replace the old terraces and vast new schools with as many pupils as Bristol University had students back at the start of the Sixties. Broadmead

7

was settling down after its rebuild in the 1950s but it stood next door to the ruins of the centre everyone had loved most of all, the blitzed Wine Street/Castle Street area; and Bristol never transferred its love to the new shops. Broadmead had ruins of the war on one side and a badly neglected St Paul's on the other. It was as if Bristol was turning its back on the old heartlands, abandoning them to decay and inner city deprivation.

Bristol was very short of ideas and the few brave sparks who did suggest that it should look to restoring its past, that people should come before cars and that cities like Bristol had a real future as places in which to live, raise families and enjoy yourself were regarded by the politicians as harmless cranks.

The big battalions were obsessed by a gigantic enterprise to carve huge roads through old Bristol. A motorway would plough through Totterdown, smash across St Augustine's Reach, bulldoze up the Clifton hillside and continues its rampaging path eastwards. The threat of it blighted whole neighbourhoods for years.

Coleridge's house in St George's Road had been demolished to clear the way for an ugly garage complex which still spoils the area around Bristol Cathedral and the Central Library. One day, shortly after I'd come to live in Bristol, a charming row of Georgian houses in Clifton, empty and supported by scaffolding, gave up the ghost and collapsed into the street. They built a multi-storey car park instead, and no-one seemed to care.

The city of a thousand trades was losing important parts of its workbase. The scores of little companies which had fed off the great industries of shipping and tobacco, aircraft and printing were dwindling. And at the heart of it all the historic harbour, the very reason why Bristol had grown in the first place, was in its death throes.

And yet . . . those same architects who designed the multi-storeys were themselves colonising old, scruffy, historic Bristol and voting with their mortgages where their hearts really lay: in treasuring the past and making it part of the future. Clifton began to shake off its raffishness as the Sixties went by and that flush of renovation spread to Cotham and Kingsdown, Redland and Bishopston. Some said it might even cross the river to Ashton and Bedminster, but that has taken a little longer.

Meanwhile a thriving social scene emerged. There were jazz clubs in pubs threatened with demolition, folk clubs in old cellars, an art gallery in an upstairs room. The Bernis showed that old Bristol could still pull 'em in and the bistros quickly followed.

The town was a wonderful stage set for the Sixties, whether it was young playwrights in Clifton garrets, rock and pop bands in the old clubs and converted warehouses or even peace and love on the Downs. It made all the mistakes of the Sixties and had all the fun and optimism of that time.

That's what this book is about, seen through the eyes of writers with a very strong affection for the place and more than a little nostalgia for that time in the city's story.

Like most of them, I came from elsewhere, was enchanted and stayed. Should I have listened to A.C.H. Smith? He recommended me as a reporter to the then editor of the *Evening Post*. The day of my interview he made me promise not to stay in Bristol after 18 months on the *Post*. 'You know what they call Bristol? The graveyard of ambition!' The pavements, they say, are softer here.

I didn't listen to him. The deadline came and went and I'm not sorry.

DAVID HARRISON
Not quite the brave new world

Where are they now, those pale half remembered ghosts of another time and another place?

Probably, like me, married and with children older than we were then. But time can freeze as well as fog the memory and Iggle, Ginge and Specs, the brilliant Summers boys and lovely Jacky with her disdainful black curls have gained a kind of immortality, preserved forever in memory as teenagers with all the ambition and emotions and arrogance that only teenage years can give.

We were quite special, of course, and we knew it. We were an experiment and because it was more of a political experiment than an educational one, we were left in no doubt of our importance.

What it is at the age of 11, after being squeezed through the sieve of the dreaded 11-plus exam, to be told the destiny of the nation rested upon our barathea-blazered shoulders. It didn't of course but more than 30 years later I can still recall the solemnity, the stirring call to arms, the sense of purpose which our black-gowned lords and masters tried to instill in us. It soon wore off. A natural cynicism about anything which adults tried to impose upon us – this was the age of rock 'n' roll, the teenage rebel and the Cold War – ensured it vanished as quickly as the elbows on our blazers.

But we retained a strong sense of being pioneers, trail-blazers in a search for a new and radical form of education that was going to give everyone the same chance to make the best of their lives. We were the green-capped army, the Davey Crocketts and Jim Bridgers of the New Jerusalem, hacking our way through the jungle of out-dated tradition and privilege, bringing succour to wasted souls cast into limbo at the age of 11 for failing the most important test in life.

Well, something like that anyway. It wasn't easy for us, facing the scorn of proper grammar school pupils and the terrible inverted snobbery of the secondary school rejects. We weren't so much pioneers of a New Jerusalem as hapless guinea pigs, willed to fail by the traditionalists and pressurised – sometimes unpleasantly – by those who needed us to succeed to prove the new system. Thankfully, the sense of irreverence inspired by Presley and James Dean – and I find it impossible to get across to my own children how dramatically the

10

attitudes of youngsters were changed by the teenage cult of the fifties and sixties – enabled most of us to survive.

I had gone to an old fashioned village school at Whitchurch which was run for a while by a sadistic couple who enjoyed caning infants and who were eventually forcibly removed when their brutality could no longer be hidden.

That apart, and we learned to avoid the vicious pair with the innate cunning of the hunted, it was a school I still remember with great affection and not just with memories rose-tinted by the passing years. We learned our tables by rote, droning them in unison; we discovered how to write, first in pencil and then – oh, joy – that marvellous day when we were trusted with a pen and inkpot. We sang stirring songs of empire and conquest like 'Hearts of Oak' and paeans of praise to obscure villains such as 'Brennan on The Moor'. Our map of the world was still largely coloured pink; we defied death by walking the parapet of the viaduct linking Whitchurch and Bristol (I am told I pale visibly at the thought as I drive across it now) and we defied the even greater reality of a painful thrashing for scrumping apples from the orchard next door. The Brabazon flew overhead and all was right with the world.

But over this idyllic existence of school plays (I once played Hansel and got into serious trouble for kissing Gretel behind the scenes and eating the ricepaper which made up the witch's house), Black Hand gangs, milk monitors and the eagerly sought privilege of ringing the dinner bell, there was always a cloud. We knew that when we reached the age of 11, we would be rigorously tested and sorted into angels and devils, sheep and goats; those destined for the upward path towards white collar jobs, mortgages and 2.4 children of our own and those doomed to clean sewers, drink in public bars and only wear a tie on Sundays. It was a prospect which terrified us all and the thought that little children should be divided into successes and failures before half of them had even begun to develop their full academic potential appals me even today.

The choice for us on the rural edge of Bristol was simple: pass and the doors of the grammar schools with their nice children, ritzy uniforms and academic excellence would open unto us and we would go up. Fail and the nearest thing to hell on earth beckoned, a secondary modern school in Knowle where, as rumour had it, the teachers were more like warders and the pupils terrorised the neighbourhood when they shambled out of their daily confinement. We heard nothing but horror stories of this school and our own experience at Jubilee baths or the Gaiety cinema of some of the Neanderthals who nominally studied there did little to lessen our fears. I was so petrified at the prospect I

11

ended up in hospital with an imaginary stomach ailment and willingly submitted to extra lessons from a hated maths teacher in a desperate bid to improve my inbred inability to recognise what numbers do and why.

The comprehensive system was designed to do away with all this. Instead of being cast into darkness at 11, all children would pass on to a comprehensive school where skilled teachers would encourage their full potential to bloom and blossom. No failures, no scrapheap, a chance of becoming a Natwest counter clerk or a double glazing salesman for all.

Of course it didn't work out like that. For a start, the system was introduced half heartedly and the traditional grammar schools were still in business and making it quite clear that they alone were the right place for the really bright child and that comprehensives were a second rate option where nice children would mix with the sort of people who had dinner at lunchtime.

I was destined for Hengrove, the second of the series of comprehensives planned around the city. My parents had naturally opted for Bristol Grammar and Bristol Cathedral as top of their list of preferences but on my urging put down Hengrove as number three. It seemed the safest move, just in case I failed and was sentenced to penal servitude in Knowle.

Despite creeping comprehensivation, I still had to take the 11-plus. Driven by absolute panic at the price of failure, I passed and moved on to discover that I wasn't at a comprehensive school at all.

Bristol education committee was so keen for the experiment to work, there was no question about the two precious comprehensive schools opening their doors to just anyone. Neither were they in fact comprehensive: what we had was a traditional grammar school and a traditional secondary modern under the same roof and the sheep and the goats were carefully divided into their respective pens on the first day.

1A and 1B: grammar streams of equal status with pupils chosen from 11-plus successes. 1C, D and E: the rest.

Equally fraudulently, there was no pretence of making it a proper neighbourhood school. Bright children were bussed in from all over the city – Stoke Bishop, Westbury-on-Trym, Clifton and even further afield. Some children faced a two hour journey each day and I often think the idea was inspired by the way the Americans tried artificially to adjust racial imbalances in schools by bussing unfortunate blacks miles each day.

Because we were a new school, two senior forms were imported from the dreaded secondary school in Knowle and proceeded to reduce the gentler newcomers, many from sheltered middle class areas of the city, to quivering jellies. Their reign of fear lasted two years and probably did irreparable damage to the cause of Socialism among several hundred impressionable youngsters.

On the first day, we stood in the newly tarmaced playground, waiting to learn our fates. All the teachers wore imposing black gowns, just like in the school stories, and almost all were graduates. No teacher training college products were to be entrusted with this first generation of the New Jerusalem: these were all good university men and women who, one presumes, believed in the new system.

We even had houses on the old public school lines, named after the city states of ancient Greece for some obscure reason (I was in Olympia, a sad choice for someone as useless at physical sports as I have always been but regarded as a bit more desirable than – snigger – Corinth). Proper uniforms were also essential, right down to the right weave of pullover for the boys and the right shade of green for the girls' gym knickers. Stupid, ludicrous green cap to be worn as far back as possible, green and silver striped tie, a dimly academic blazer badge, a blazer which invariably looked old and shabby within a week of buying it – how has such an unsuitable outfit for energetic, dirty children ever lasted so long?

Our lessons in the grammar streams were exactly the same as if we had been at a separate grammar school. We did the basics plus French, German, Latin, and sciences and the usual esoteric extras, and from day one we were in training for the next hurdle on the steeplechase of life: the GCE O Level.

We were not encouraged to mix with the lower, less academic forms. It wasn't actually banned so much as disapproved. Social experimentation was fine but there were limits and great things were expected of us.

In true public school fashion – we had all read the books – everyone had to have a nick-name. For some reason, we decided to call everyone by their second names if they had one, and after physical characteristics if they didn't. So I was Bill which was a small cross to bear and thus were born Ginge, Specs and Iggle – the latter a sullen, powerful boy who revelled in his amazing covering of body hair and was prone to disastrous outbursts of violent temper when pushed too far. He's probably in public relations now.

On the whole, the teachers were a decent bunch. Corky, the affable and popular English teacher who instilled in me a love of the language; Yogi Green, the irascible chemistry expert whom I infuriated by accidentally breathing in some of the chlorine I had just made ('Stupid child, make some ammonia and that will neutralise it' he screamed as I

13

collapsed in agony); an ex-Spitfire pilot who taught French and favoured the pretty girls in the class; Dr Perry, the ascetic head who always seemed slightly out of place in a modern building without columns and pediments.

There were one or two who didn't rank so well – a ludicrous sporting show-off prone to demonstrating his ball control where the maximum number could see him; a rather undistinguished little man who was invited to teach elsewhere after some sixth-formers caught him providing extra lessons to our resident dumb blonde; the usual rampagers and roarers who appear in any school. But on the whole, I feel in retrospect we were very well served and I have a genuine gratitude for the wide interests and inquiring nature which Hengrove awoke in me.

The school was never truly comprehensive while I was there but there were moments of great rejoicing for its supporters. I well recall one girl who failed her 11-plus so badly she ended up in the lowest stream of the lowest class. At the age of 13 or 14, her intellect seemed to awake from a sleep and she was transferred to the highest stream. She left with more O and A levels than anyone else and headed for a distinguished career in nuclear physics. On the other hand, there were those chosen at 11 but whose potential seemed to burn out quickly and who were rapidly exiled to avoid polluting the rest of us.

We had some unlikely special pressures on us, too, throughout our time there. We were hauled over the coals for lying in an untidy, mixed-sex heap on the playing fields at lunchtime because neighbouring houses could see and would get the wrong idea. We had to wear correct uniform at all times, behave impeccably on buses, let people know we were at a Good School. It didn't always work: we were taught the art of heckling when the school was invited to an inter-school debating competition with the grammar schools and learned it so enthusiastically we had to be reined in in mid-debate. But we held our own in such traditional activities as sports and public speaking, which is not really surprising considering that many of our pupils were hand-picked from across Bristol.

GCE time and the thumbscrews were applied. It was not just us but the system on trial and a satisfying number of fourth formers had already gained one or two early O-levels, just like they did in the real grammar schools.

Imagine the horror of the maths exam, however, when it dawned on even our brightest stars that they didn't understand half the questions, let alone the answers. A feeling of panic and gloom spread quickly round the room, until even the presiding master noticed. Sadly, he wasn't a mathematician or the whole farce might have ended sooner. It

14

wasn't until we were gathered in despair afterwards, the mediocre like me taking comfort from the downfall of the brilliant, that we were told we had been set the wrong paper and that the questions demanded knowledge not usually acquired until the upper sixth. We all took the exam again at Christmas and the results were good enough to keep everyone happy.

There was more pressure to stay on into the sixth form, and as most of us hadn't the slightest idea what we wanted to do in life, it seemed a reasonable idea. So we did, living two pleasant years as kings and queens of the roost, arguing about the merits of Miles Davis (then a surprising cult among teenagers); about Buddy Holly's best songs and Dylan Thomas' poetry; about the point of learning Latin and why the Germans had such ponderous compound words. We formed liaisons, we were allowed to wear civvies instead of uniforms, we smoked without ever inhaling because no one could do it without choking; we organised dance classes to learn the social graces. We prowled around in drainpipes and bumfreezer jackets and boasted in our own argot of mythical sexual encounters and last night's illegal drinking session at the jazz club in Redcliffe Hill ('Hiawatha Rag' was our most requested number, so requested in fact the band requested – ordered, demanded – we leave). And we studied on and off in our own private sixth form quarters formed by walling off the ends of two large classrooms.

It was a large sixth form and an artificially good one, and I think the teachers and politicians had great hopes for us. A very large percentage went on to university – more than most comprehensives could dream of now, I think – and I was very coldly greeted when I announced that I had been offered a job as trainee on a weekly paper and would be studying at college on day release instead of trying for a proper university place. I was left with the impression I was letting down the side a bit and I must admit there are times I have regretted my stubbornness.

Hengrove has changed, like all other comprehensives. Now it is truly comprehensive, a neighbourhood school drawing children from a logical area rather than across the city. The debate goes on, the grammar schools survive contrary to all the forecasts, the inequality is now governed by wealth rather than ability. Iggle, Ginger, Specs and me, we were part of a brave dream that never really turned into reality and probably never will. But still I remember Janice, the 11-plus failure who walked away with all the prizes after she was written off. She, too, is frozen in memory as a pretty 18 year old and I have no idea where she is or what she achieved in adult life. But she had the chance and for her and people like her, I still feel glad that we went some way along the road towards the New Jerusalem together.

ROSALIND ANSTEY

Those were the days, my friend

'Those were the days my friend' sang Mary Hopkins in the Sixties and they were . . . golden, halcyon days when our main aim in life was making enough money to keep us in fashion to attract boys. Working for Ralph Edwards, architect, DID NOT yield a good wage, although I did get to serve tea and biscuits – soggy ones – to Reece Winstone, about to embark on publication of his first Bristol book. 'Of course I remember you, my dear' he wrote years later.

MONEY I wanted, so to the Northern Insurance Company I went, each morning winding my way between cases of fruit spilling onto Queen Charlotte Street, tottering on my 6″ stilettos trying to avoid bananas and rotting cabbage leaves, finally coming-to in Caroline's Cake shop after a strong black coffee and a fag. Haring round the corner, past the half finished Rank-Xerox building with the sound of wolfwhistles and 'Hey Dusty' in my ears I would stagger up the steps and fall into the all-hallowed arms of The Company to make MONEY and watch Stan pick his nose discreetly, or so he thought, at the back of the office. Tea-breaks would find us comparing notes on the night before, with Joan continually falling in love with different aspiring actors who boarded with her aunt. Once it was an Irish one named Peter O'Toole.

Dinner hours would be spent in coffee bars: the Cona-cadet, where the Ancient Independent Order of Foresters kept us amused with their anecdotes, once narrowly missing the Supremes who had decided to dine there in their large picture hats while appearing at the Colston Hall; and the Bolero in Queen's Road, where the exciting, dimly-lit basement would invite us down the stairs, the swishing, hissing of the espresso coffee and the wafting smell of blue Gauloise cigarettes leading us to exciting Latin boys. Or we would shop for clothes in the newly opened C & A Mode keeping us up to date with fashion. We once watched Fairfax House burning while onlookers ate their sandwiches, the flames racing through the top floor in seconds.

And so to getting boys . . . you would often see us perched on a wall on the Centre, watching LIFE (and local talent) go by. When we saw Acker Bilk and Tommy Bruce approaching us in their Teddyboy suits we hid, too shy to ask for autographs. Seeing them later at the Colston

Hall, we kicked ourselves. We saw many good acts there including half of the Everly Brothers, Roy Orbison, a black solitary figure with a voice of pure gold, Buddy Holly, who chuffed us no end when he thanked us for the toffees we threw on his drums, Gene Vincent mean and moody in black, Bee Bumble and the Stingers (Bee Bumble who?), but we didn't get tickets to see Eddie Cochran, much to our eternal regret.

And so to getting boys. . . Dances could be the answer. After an initial course at the Sydenham School of Dancing, 'experts in Cha-cha, Samba' and a sedate version of the jive, we were ready. We descended on the Glen. Girls frantically back-combed their hair with the aid of Miners Hair Lacquer, chattering excitedly in front of gilded mirrors. In the ballroom, a huge sparkling globe spun around on the ceiling, casting images of girls bopping away in their flat, ballerina shoes and Chanel-style suits, images of the future Darth Vader (Dave Prowse) leaning against the wall waiting for trouble, his giant body crammed into a dark suit and his hornrimmed glasses hiding his eyes. Joining the Tudor Club in the Glen, we queued for over an hour to see the latest phenomenon Shane Fenton, finally coming face to face with a bored young fair-haired man who hurriedly signed the bits of paper clutched in our hot little hands. I much preferred the dark haired Alvin Stardust he later became. The Chinese Jazz Club on a Tuesday sported a huge dance floor with shadowy alcoves around the edges where students and their girlfriends earnestly put the world to rights between dances. Uncle Bonny, in his straw boater and clutching joss sticks, would wander round keeping us in order. We saw many good bands there including Alexis Korner with Charlie Watts, later of the Stones, on drums, Dick Charlesworth with singer Jeannie Lamb were favourites while Terry Lightfoot appeared, once chatting me up at half time in the Rummer. Pete Budd (later of the Wurzels), with whom I spent a whole evening discussing Fats Domino in the Hart at Bris, and Johnny Carr and the Cadillacs graced our outlying villages with dances. Johnny Carr even asked me to dance but I declined. He seemed a bit condescending . . . sorry Johnny (or should I say Cornelius?) . . . another time? The Riccoco Club, a little Club approached from Leonards Lane, also kept us dancing. We would squeeze down dark corridors, finally reaching the smoky arched cellar and Avon Cities Jazz Band with their girl singer who we saw years later busking at Clifton. During the University Rag we would follow the jazz band to an island by Neptune's statue, there to dance the night away while the band played in their duffle coats and scarves.

And so to getting boys. . . The cinema was not such a good way of getting boys, but alright if you already had one. During the 60s this part of courtship suffered as many of the cinemas closed to re-open as bingo halls, starting with the Savoy at Shire where I once knitted the back of a jumper during *Giant* with James Dean (no, James Dean did not help me knit my jumper). Even the Ritz succumbed to closure after helping me find my 'True Love'. The Tatler, with its dirty mac brigade occupying a couple of rows, saw us through our foreign film phase when we fell in love with a German unknown with seductive eyes. He didn't look so seductive in *The Magnificent Seven* but in *Tiger Bay* we again loved Horst Bucholz.

And so to getting boys. . . Roma's hairstyles at Bedminster would see us on a Friday night suffering for fashion. . . The Black Tulip dye would run out as we all rushed through like a factory assembly line getting our hair bouffanted for the weekend. In would go individuals and out would come Cilla Black clones. How we suffered under those dryers reading our *Honey* magazines (I read *Vogue*) and how I suffered trying to strain my unruly blonde curls into the straight bob of Cilla's . . . even a Mary Quant style would have been nice . . . but a Dusty Springfield style wasn't so bad and the boys seemed to like it so who was I to complain? But I did suffer trying . . . reading my *Vogue* and lusting after clothes I couldn't afford, making do with the old Singer treadle machine at home making shift dresses and A-line skirts.

And so to getting boys . . . pubs perhaps were the answer. The Llandoger Trow, smelling of sherry, didn't yield much in the way of boys, only married men. We would watch the students at the Somerset in Park Row waving their arms about, heatedly putting the world to rights. . . Utopia became a popular word. I would wear my large, black floppy hat in the style of Rembrandt as I tried to fit in . . . I didn't but the landlady said I looked good so . . . eat your heart out, George Melly. Courtney, the landlord, would bore us to tears giving the weather report from all over England and then starting on the traffic reports. One day, to shut him up, one of our student friends locked poor Courtney in his cellar. We *did* meet two rare boys there, Pepe with his fake Spanish accent and trainee engineer Mike. Yippee . . . we were going to our first student party at Cotham . . . and then they had a whip-round for a bottle of cider. We should have taken the hint. It stayed at one bottle of cider, all evening. Eventually we left. The Ostrich, with its footprints across the ceiling, held me enthralled one evening while trying to get off with a handsome boy. I got off alright, even though the footprints got wavier as I mixed my drinks. I made it to the door . . . just. I never did see him again. The White Lion at Portishead produced sailors and one evening, I had a date with a Belgian sailor called Ernest. He turned up and so did the entire crew of the Leon Dens. They thought I could help them find some girls. Oh

God, where on earth do I find girls? An hour later saw a crocodile of Belgian sailors crossing the Centre led by me and Ernest. I'd heard that the Holborn Caff in Denmark Street was a 'den of vice', so picking our way through the Nortons, Road Rockets, BSAs and one 1000cc Vincent parked outside, in we went. They gawped, their mouths staying open. Ernest and I left . . . without the crew of the Leon Dens. Phew ! ! ! The Greyhound also was a good place to meet boys. We would pose in one of the many doorways, a glass of lukewarm Devenish bitter in our hands, fluttering our eyes. The Rummer and Cellar Bars were even better. The Rummer had lots of dimly lit bars underground with glass balls hanging in nets from the ceiling. Our friend Janet would serve glasses of sherry and collect tip after tip. How we envied her. We spied Patrick Troughton, minus his Doctor Who scarf, earnestly engaged in conversation with some dubious looking friends and even Charles Gray spoke to us one night. We declined an offer of a ride under the Suspension Bridge in a balloon, missed out on a ski-ing invitation from some so-say television producers and met the RAF most Wednesday nights for a chat. The Cellar Bar was a little rougher but you did meet boys, even if it was just a squeeze in the tightly packed cellar. There would be the odd fight thrown in with eight teddyboys one night escaping into a bubble car, *shutting the door* and driving off without the aid of a periscope. The Radnor with its nightly parade of pretty men was of no use to us whatsoever while the Hole in the Wall was strictly for Christmas office drinks. The Bear and Rugged Staff saw us nearly knocked out by a Teddyboy who came flying through the air at 90 miles an hour at the end of someone's fist. At Dunlops we were invited aboard a submarine which just happened to be visiting Bristol. We declined of course, being modest young maidens. And at the Old Duke we spent many a happy night being squeezed to death and listening to our favourite jazz.

If we did happen to find a boy we would go on to supper at the Steak and Stilton, Rummer or Llandoger Trow, all three being romantic, softly-lit places with candles placed discreetly at the tables. Or it would be the Posada where you could get a fried egg on top of your steak for the same 7/6d. But we liked the Tavern at Queens Road where you could watch the world go by through a little, tunnelled entrance. If there was a gang of us we would all pile down St. John's Lane to Stan's, where they did a lovely Clark's pie and chips. Teddyboys and Mods would queue in orderly rows and came from miles around to sample Stan's wares. Many a letterbox in St John's Lane suffered an influx of unwanted green peas. Chinese restaurants were beginning and we couldn't wait to visit the Four Seas where, it was said, a Chinese waiter had run amok with a machete. If we didn't go for a meal it was coffee at the Bali in Union Street, where one night we saw a young man grovelling on the floor. He was finishing off his 'stag night' and had missed the step, ending up in a crumpled heap beneath our table. 'Here Val, isn't that John of John and Julie?', I asked. 'I think you're right, Ros. He is getting married tomorrow'. He later got thrown out for being drunk. When I play my Blue Mink L.P. I often think of Roger Cook lying in a crumpled heap beneath our table.

And so to getting boys . . . weekends we tried but weren't successful. We even ventured down to Sheppard's Teagardens at Saltford where we heard boys would come from all over Bristol, grab a boat and maybe, for the sheer hell of it, dive into the river fully clothed. I never saw any of this until I finally met my 'True Love', courtesy of the Ritz, and then I was part of that scene, one of the girls in summery dresses sitting on the riverbank while our boyfriends dried out their 10/- notes, their Billy Fury-styled collars standing above their jackets which sported little three cornered, imitation hankies in their top pockets.

Those were the days indeed, Mary Hopkins . . . and I wouldn't have changed them for the world.

HELEN REID
Liberated, after a fashion

For me, there is one enduring image of the Sixties. It is a memory of a Women's Institute bazaar, held on a Somerset vicarage lawn, circa 1969. The good ladies are taking tea with the vicar, and are wearing the expected tweed suits and Crimplene dresses beloved of their kind.

The extraordinary thing is that they are all wearing mini-length skirts. This uniform of the Swinging Sixties had percolated through to the bastions of rural life, and women of all classes and age groups (except perhaps the Queen) had bared their knees, suitably or otherwise.

For me that sums up the Sixties: women had been conned. It was supposed to be the great decade of youth and liberation and permissiveness, but it was all centred on the hemline. Underneath their short skirts, women went on much as before. They got paid less for doing the same job as a man, had to get their husbands' permission to work, borrow money, or take out a hire-purchase agreement, and they were still terrified of getting pregnant.

The Sixties was a schizoid time for women: theoretically they were living in the affluent permissive age of the Pill, so why were they so depressed and ultimately angry about their lot? As early as 1964, the Married Women's Association called for legal financial partnership for wives, and there were complaints that there were no women working in the Stock Exchange.

The double standards of the day became evident in the notorious 'kiss and cuddle' case that year: a newly-wed couple were caught by a policeman having a torrid encounter in their car and were charged with outraging decency by committing 'a lewd, obscene and disgusting act.' They were acquitted – but SHE lost her job.

To begin at the beginning of the decade, I got married in 1960, wearing I may add, a Crimplene dress and jacket.

I was before my time in that I was the sole breadwinner, though of course there was no question of role reversal. I still did all the housework, shopping and cooking. So birth control was very necessary: women who had babies in 1960 did not go back to work, and we would have starved. So a week or so before the wedding, I went to the Charlotte Keil Clinic in Easton for family planning advice. It was all rather furtive.

'When are you getting married?' asked the FP lady. Where are you getting married? What are you going to wear? How many are coming to the reception? Where are you going for your honeymoon?

I couldn't see for the life of me what this had to do with birth control, but it gradually dawned on me that the FP lady was checking up to see if I was genuinely going to get married, or whether I planned to live in sin. If you lived in sin in the early 1960's, they wouldn't issue you with any birth control supplies. Only married women were allowed to have safe sex. For unsafe sex, you relied on male contraception, or the very bold sneaked into Madame Pierre's in Denmark Street. Girls who played around were MEANT to be punished by pregnancy in those pre-Pill days.

The Pill came along in 1964, significantly at the same time as the mini skirt, but it hardly changed things overnight. For a start, it was very hard for an unmarried female to get supplies, and the Sixties was the era of gymslip mums, as they were called. I remember talking to a group of them in a hostel for unwed mothers in St. Pauls, and these girls knew nothing about contraception. They had got the message about the Swinging Sixties and permissiveness, but were not allowed to go on the Pill. Backstreet abortions were available in Bedminster, it was rumoured.

In any case, there were worries about the safety of the Pill, and when it was prescribed, doctors and clinics liked to get the husband's permission. Moreover, the Pill was no help to the poor mothers of big families: it was not available on the NHS.

Sexual liberation was a big issue in the Sixties, but it was more talked about than practised; the risks were still too high. We were all great theorists of freedom, banging on about equal rights and equal pay, and moaning about the injustice of housework at home, but we just grumbled, and did nothing about it.

This was the decade of the Miserable Married Women, and women journalists were constantly writing about mothers who complained they were imprisoned in their homes, and that their brains were rotting because of motherhood. The Housebound Housewives Register and the Graduates Register were set up to put lonely miserable mothers in touch with one another and stretch their minds by talking about subjects that had nothing to do with home or babies. Depression was the keynote; this was the period when women started taking to tranquillisers in a big way.

Whispers of women's liberation were arriving, but it was a long way off, mainly for economic reasons. Women began to grasp the fact that without economic power, they would never get anywhere.

The key to that economic power was a job, but when men married in the Sixties, they would still say: 'No wife of mine is ever going to work'. The idea of working when you had young children was anathema – Spock and Bowlby had brainwashed us with theories of maternal deprivation, and there were scandals about latch-key kids.

So only a small minority of married women worked full time, three million compared with nine million now, and this had its effect on what we would call now sexual politics. Women were not expected to achieve high office or executive status, and when they did, we journalists would buzz round like bees to interview these fabulous rare beasts. Just imagine, a woman bank manager!

My editor of the day had a fairly typical attitude. When pay rises were handed out, he would say: 'You're married, you've got a husband to support you, you don't need more money. I have married men on my staff who have a family to keep and a mortgage to pay, and if there is any money around it must go to them.' He was an MCP long before the term was invented. And proud of it.

Looking back on the women's page articles I wrote then, I'm astonished to see how limited the scope was; so much about homes and babies and knitting and fashion, so little about real issues. Often I would interview women whose sole claim to fame was that they had famous or important husbands. And I would ask them about their clothes!

I used to go around giving talks to women's organisations about my job; when the questions came, they were about how I managed to reconcile my career with being married and a housewife as well, and they seemed to be far more interested in my domestic arrangements than my work. The problem still exists but now it is viewed from the other end of the telescope: how do you reconcile your domestic life with your career?

Yet towards the end of the decade, consciousness was being raised, if only an inch above the kitchen sink. I remember interviewing a group of Redland women who had decided to live in a commune, because they were disillusioned with men and marriage and thought women were easier and kinder to live with.

It never crossed my mind that they were lesbians, and I don't think they were. In any case it was immaterial because the word would not have been printed. It was banned in the WDP, like the word 'period', as in the Georgian period. 'No menstrual allusions,' said the Editor. The polite word to use was 'era'.

One turning point, greatly trivialised at the time, was the legendary bra-burning episode which was supposed to have taken place in Atlantic City, in the USA in 1968. A group of women had a demo, protesting about the Miss America contest taking place there. They said it enforced a stereotype of femininity that debased women and packaged them into sex objects. The bra, emblem of a false femininity, controlled and packaged, was the symbol of that stereotype, and they burnt it.

The media went wild and bra-burning became a national joke: you had only to express the slightest feminist sentiment to a man for him to chuckle Ho, ho, I suppose you're a bra-burner. Women who did believe in equality became very defensive: they'd say in interviews: 'Of course I'm not a women's libber, but. . .' It wasn't a label that the average women wanted to be branded with.

It was the frustration and anger about the lack of progress for women that finally led in April 1969 to the formation of the first women's liberation group in Bristol, started by Clifton lecturer Ellen Malos. Most of the meetings were held in her home. The first was to arrange for a coachload of Bristol women to go to an Equal Pay demo in London. The group also collected signatures for a petition, in Broadmead, and protested at the 1969 Miss World contest. (In October that year, Barbara Castle, then Secretary of State for Social Services, promised Equal Pay by 1975.)

'They were a mixed bunch of women, and by no means all middle-class,' she recalls. 'Some had jobs, some were working in the arts, some were housewives, and they were mostly in their twenties and thirties. There were no students interested in feminism at that stage. We were enraged by all the superficial talk of equality, when all the evidence was against it.

'The things we discussed in those early meetings were the obvious ones: the battle for equal pay and equal opportunities, contraception, the problems of unmarried mothers, the need for women to have control over their own fertility. It was the beginning of the pressure that finally brought about the Equal Pay Act in 1975. We got out a roughly roneoed manifesto called **Enough!** and the first issue was entitled "The Patriarchal Family – Refuge or Prison?"'

Another milestone was the first meeting of the Wages For Housework Campaign, in 1969. For a group of women were proposing a mind-blowing idea: that women should actually be paid for what they were apparently created to do, i.e. clean lavatories, make soup and change nappies. It was the first time that I clearly realised that for women, as for men, money was power, and that economic power was one of the keys to equality. Then I went home to cook (unpaid) the supper.

But what every woman remembers about the Sixties were the fashions: it was an ultra-fashion conscious decade.

That great symbol of the Sixties, the mini-skirt, was a perfect example of the ambiguity of the position of women in Swinging Britain. (Not that Bristol exactly swung; fashion was still at least a year behind the excesses of the Carnaby Street boutiques.)

There had been an explosion of youth culture: the post-war bulge produced a new generation of young consumers who at last had money, and they wanted to spend it on fashion that proclaimed they were a new wave, quite different from their dull, prim fifties predecessors.

Mary Quant started it all, with her Chelsea girl look, a total reaction from the staid maidenly Fifties girl who wore long full skirts, white gloves, had a tiny waist, and a tiny constricted mind to go with it. The New Girl was free, independent and sexually liberated and she said so via her clothes, or so she thought.

The first minis arrived in 1964 and proceeded up through the decade from knee length to mid thigh. Tights had to be invented to hide the suspender gap. (I remember interviewing Mary Quant in 1964 when she promised she had revolutionary solutions to that pressing female problem, the suspender bump.) That mini skirts were impractical, freezing in winter and an embarrassment to those with porky legs, was not mentioned. Girls used to complain about open-tread staircases, with good reason.

As 1970 approached, clothes got more and more outrageous; hot pants for work, see-through blouses, and dresses made in openwork crochet with strategic solid bits in the dangerous regions. The ultimate was the topless dress, and – joy for the media – we could photograph girls wearing them, with their arms modestly folded in front of their bared bosoms.

But with hindsight, it is obvious that the mini was not in the least liberating: it was just a new and very sexist uniform that turned women into sex objects who had to be very careful about the way they moved and sat. The message was totally contradictory: I'm showing you almost all I've got, but I'm not available.

The Swinging Sixties ethos persuaded not just young girls but mature women to dress up like dolls. Even official uniforms were mini, and women working in jobs where a mini-skirt was a positive hazard, traffic wardens, policewomen, air hostesses, service-women, nurses, all followed suit. I interviewed a policewoman who had been appointed the first-ever Chief Inspector in the city, and even she was wearing a uniform mini-skirt.

For the extraordinary paradox is that the fashions of the Sixties, meant to proclaim liberation and freedom, actually turned grown women into little girls. They were even known as dollybirds, and bought dresses known as Dollyrockers, from J. F. Taylor's.

The Sixties girl was thin, flat-chested, narrow-shouldered, and pale faced, with big sooty eyes; she had long skinny legs and a round Sassooned head, just like a doll. Slimming was terribly important in the Sixties, and very much part of the desire not to grow up and look mature, because only young girls were supposed to have the fun. Women's pages were always featuring miraculous slimming feats, and the shrunken victor invariably cried: 'At last I can wear a mini.'

The dresses the Sixties girl wore were really children's clothes scaled up; she wore smocks and empire line dresses with ruffles and tucks, and baby doll nighties and outfits like rompers, and little strap shoes with pointed toes. Far from presenting herself as a free woman, she presented herself as a toy, a Twiggy.

The young men's fashions had the same infantilism about them: the Beatles with their long basin-cut hair and neat little jackets were aping childhood fashion. It was not a grown-up decade and the fashions echoed this.

A revolt did come at the end of the decade, with the flower children's hippy garb, the ethnic look, and a gradual realisation amongst women that they had been conned into mini-skirted conformity. Women's liberation was about breaking away from stereotypes of femininity and clothes were a powerful expression of this urge. The students sat-in at Bristol University, women marched against the Bomb, and the childishness of the Sixties came to an end. Not before time.

GEORGE FERGUSON
The high rise, concrete city

Arriving in Bristol twenty years after the end of the second World war, as I did, one would be forgiven for thinking that hostilities had finished only a few years earlier. In some ways it could be said this was when hostilities began. I came to Bristol as an architectural student, wide-eyed and ready for the excitement of this big, strange city. They were heady days – we never had it so good – and I hurtled into Bristol for the first time by the Wells Road and Three Lamps junction. The cast iron Bath & Wells finger post has remained ever since my symbol of Bristol's changed fortunes. I did not imagine as I passed the terraces of Totter-down that hundreds of these houses and a whole city centre community would disappear by the end of the decade, but then I did not know how the planning of Bristol was in the grip of highway engineers with more regard for Los Angeles-style spaghetti junctions and urban motorways than for the traditions and the people of a rich and varied city.

Bristol in the 1960's was dominated by two powerful but misguided local politicians, Alderman Wally Jenkins and Alderman Gervais Walker, one Labour, one Conservative, but to all intents and purposes the same. Wags dubbed them Wally Walker and Gervais Jenkins. It was these two, and their apparent resolve to destroy the best of Bristol, that was eventually to drive me briefly into the planning department and into the local politics of the seventies.

So I drove innocently on into Bristol in my pre-MOT Morris 8, bought for a tenner, and generously or stupidly sold later on for the same. I passed bomb sites and derelict buildings, some covered in buddleia, known locally as 'blitz weed', through the decayed elegance of Clifton and up to the brand new Students Union, standing a symbol of the brave new world rising above the peeling paint and decaying roofs of its surrounding terraces. Immediately christened the Students Hilton, it was more interesting to me for the length of its bar than the quality of its architecture. These were arrogant times, when architects, planners, and politicians alike seemed blind to the qualities of the past which were seen as little more than a hindrance to the plans for the future. The process was made so much easier by the total absence of any public consultation and the consequent passive submission of most of the population.

So from my place of play to my place of work; the architectural school in Washington House on Brandon Hill – surely one of Bristol's greatest eyesores ever – which as I write 25 years on is thankfully being replaced with a more appropriate building. The concrete greed of Washington House may have gone (we thought it was falling down even when we were students), but the legacy of the commercial boom of the 1960's remains. It was a period when Bristol did its best to obliterate what Hitler had left behind in the ancient Lewins Mead, for example, and replace it with concrete towers and concrete walkways. These windswept viaducts were to take the pedestrians above the traffic, to enable it to race unimpeded round the new inner circuit road.

Segregation was designed to make pedestrians second class citizens, windswept on high level pedestrian walkways, or attacked in subways before mugging became endemic. This traffic 'utopia' nearly succeeded, but the highway planners were thwarted by the end of the commercial boom and by growing public anger. Sadly, the highway men had time to complete the circle, cutting diagonally through Britain's largest square and leaving St. Mary Redcliffe, Elizabeth I's 'fairest parish church', to an ignominious future bounded by dual carriageways and a vast traffic roundabout. Some objectors said such an exquisite building might as well be put out of its agony and demolished. This extremism represented a desperate cry for help by the valiant few 'eccentric aesthetes' who felt powerless in the face of the elected dinosaur.

But Bristol's highway men had more in store: a fantastic plan which was essential, we were told, to the city's future prosperity. The Outer Circuit Road was to be an urban motorway that linked all the main radial routes into Bristol and overcame that inconvenient barrier to traffic: the historic floating harbour. The City Engineer, James Bennett, had shown the way with his great swing bridge at Cumberland Basin and his flyover, Bennett Way, that cut its way mercilessly into early Georgian Hotwells. This was nothing compared with what was planned. Swing bridges were expensive to build and operate. The plot was to close the City Docks, to compensate the dockside industries, most notably Hills Dockyards, and to build another spaghetti junction to straddle the City Docks where the s.s. Great Britain now lies. The outer circuit road became 'make or break' for me as far as Bristol was concerned. If we stopped it, it was a place worth living in. If we let it happen it deserved its reputation as being one of the most philistine cities of philistine Britain in the sixties.

From crossing the City Docks, this urban motorway was to straddle Brandon Hill, tunnel into the Clifton slopes, re-emerge at a massive

28

junction behind the Victoria Rooms, tear its way through Tyndalls Park and Cotham Hill, skirt Georgian Kingsdown and dive straight through St Pauls to connect to the roundabout at the end of the M32. From here a single mile actually got built in the early 1970's, running to the Lawrence Hill roundabout, between the 17-storey blocks of Easton flats designed by the then City Architect as 'an impressive entrance to the city'. From here the Outer Circuit Road was to fly through Barton Hill and St Philips to join a massive new multi-level junction on the site of the demolished terraces of Totterdown. It was then to descend through Bedminster and complete the circuit of destruction back to the City Docks.

This lunatic plan – part of the 1966 Development Plan – was still very much alive in the early 1970's in spite of growing opposition and one might think it had almost been planned to taunt the trendier parts of Bristol. If so it certainly succeeded in doing so, and by the early seventies Bristol's politicians could never again plan on the grand scale without some degree of consent.

Bristol has a reputation for being cautious and marketing men say that if you can sell in Bristol you can sell anywhere. What was surprising maybe was that the national planning trends of the time were accepted with such enthusiasm by the city's ruling clique. This, of course, extended to enthusiasm for high rise blocks of flats; the simple solution to slum clearance with the added attraction of fine views and fresh air. My profession had unwittingly given the politicians a brave new solution that could be stripped of its Corbusian dream of a self-contained community in the sky to become a cynical numbers game. A statistic now almost completely lost from popular politics is that of new council homes (or of 'units' as they were so often suitably called). In the sixties this was an election statistic as important as unemployment or the trade balance.

Bristol was not to be left out. Now bored with the relentless rows of fifties' council housing, the planners turned to the high rise block, from which no part of the city was safe. There was not a squeak of protest from the new suburbs like Hartcliffe, but horror from some when it came to the hillsides of Kingsdown and Cliftonwood. Kingsdown succumbed with three massive council blocks destroying the grain of development both in plan and elevation. The new Dove Street flats were cut into a hillside that had previously been developed along its contours. This was 'set square' architecture using the gridline of the ordnance survey map in preference to the elegant streets and squares of Georgian Kingsdown. The Hospital Board was to continue to demonstrate that insensitive development does not necessarily stem from greed, but also from the misguided belief that it is simpler to maintain a single-minded approach to social problems without complicating them with the subtleties of urban design.

The Cliftonwood hillside was more fortunate: an even more bizarre plan was afoot to demolish that hillside of delightful artisan houses (with the advantage that they could be bought by the brave or the foolish for a few hundred pounds), to replace then with three more massive multi-storey blocks incorporating escalators to take people from Hotwells Road to upper Clifton. That nightmare did not materialise, although new flats were built at the Jacobs Wells roundabout.

The blocks that were built will for many years remain as monuments to the insensitivity of the sixties but they will, mercifully, be long outlived by the terraces of traditional houses which escaped the bulldozer.

The physical and visual change was nothing to the social disaster caused by the loss of street communities and the stranding of mothers and children in high rise flats.

If we had apparently produced a formula for solving the housing crisis we had also provided developers with an excuse to build large areas of offices as cheaply as possible. Ornament was still an architectural crime in the sixties, and developers were able to replace some of Bristol's most decorative and characteristic buildings with system-built structures and higher plot ratios. The city engineer and planning officer had agreed to bumping up the plot ratio to satisfy the developers' insatiable desire for square footage so long as more parking could be provided. 'More people in more cars' became the five-word transport policy of the time. The centre was for working in and the suburbs for living in and everyone was to get into their car between 8 and 9 in the morning, park it in the city centre and return home between 5 and 6 in the evening.

The extreme example of the city's enthusiasm for this policy was an office development on venerable Welsh Back. The developers approached the planners with a proposal for an 8-storey office building. They were promised the go-ahead, if only they could slip six storeys of car parking underneath it. The developers simply raised the office building over the car parking and planning permission was duly granted. The extraordinary result is there for all to see.

The multi-storey car park was one of the main features of the plans for Bristol in the sixties. The dreaded initials MSCP would appear over the top of Georgian terraces, such as Berkeley Place, at Frogmore Street and at various points in and around the inner circuit road.

However, I would be doing a disservice to the sixties and my memory of those years to leave the impression that this decadence was

30

confined to planning. In other spheres it ran just as deep. The Californian influence of 'living for today' may have wrecked a few cities and contributed to the environmental problems that haunt us today, but it was fun while it lasted. The future seemed so promising with nuclear power generated electricity so cheap that it would not be worth billing; and planning for leisure, as robots and computers were to take time consuming drudgery out of human hands.

This planning for a future of leisure was epitomised by the Mecca Entertainment Centre in Frogmore Street, which wiped out one of Bristol's most varied historic areas in favour of a barbaric mixture of brick, concrete and neon lights. No quarter was given to those who stood in the way of progress and comprehensive redevelopment. The punishment was a pittance in compensation and a flat in a Hartcliffe high-rise.

But by the end of the sixties Bristolians began to wake up. It would take the best part of the seventies, though, for the establishment to realise that Bristol is a place to be nurtured, not butchered.

JAMES BELSEY

Concorde

Think of symbols of the Sixties and there she is, sleek, slim, pale: Concorde. The world's great airports like Heathrow and Kennedy should be her natural habitat but she looks curiously out of place, like a whey-faced, Twiggy-slim Mod dolly bird from long-departed boutiques. Concorde: an incongruously small, fey creature towered above by today's more prosaic, functional workhorses of the sky, the great jumbos and the huge airbuses.

That very name Concorde – full of Sixties' optimism, some might say blind faith. It signifies peace and harmony and it is wholly inappropriate. Concorde was born from an uneasy Anglo-French marriage in which harmony was often lacking and, as for peace, stand beneath Concorde's flight path as she makes her final descent over London to reach Heathrow. All that noise so that a few score people can cross the Atlantic a few hours faster than the rest of us?

The twentieth anniversary of Concorde's maiden flights fell recently and it proved an eerie celebration. The ghosts of twenty years ago were heard again, the persuaders and the publicists, press acolytes and sycophants with their chorus of unquestioning superlatives. Isn't she lovely, isn't she daring, isn't she an inspiration? No room for doubt, no moments of thoughtful reflection. The Concorde myth and mystique is as potent as ever and it is enshrined not just in Bristol or even British mythology, but in the minds of the world: That here is beauty and daring and technology wedded in a single, wonderful object. I'm sorry. Beauty is what beauty does and in many ways Concorde is a perfect symbol of the fizzy, silly, snobby, arrogant world they called The Swinging Sixties. My Dad's Got A Jensen Interceptor, a particularly offensive Sixties' advertisement sneered. My Dad's gone one better . . . he's flown on Concorde!

Bristol's post-war planemakers had a marvellously ambitious streak and we loved them for it. First they built the Brabazon, the world's biggest plane, but she proved hopelessly slow, an underpowered ocean liner of the sky. Next came Britannia, a truly lovely plane which deserved a far better fate than the one she suffered. She was dogged by delays and ill-luck, and a crash on a publicity flight cost the programme a couple of years. When she did arrive, it was too late. Britannia was smooth, quiet and reliable, but she was prop-driven and by then the airlines knew that the world's first big, profitable intercontinental jetliner, the Boeing 707, lay just around the corner. They made do with their old transports until the 707 was available.

Bristol's planemakers did very well with at least one line, the famous Bristol Freighters. Some are still in service today, doing a grand job fetching and carrying goods cheaply and efficiently, which is what the best commercial aircraft are supposed to do. But Bristol hungered for something more dashing. The Filton team were itching to join the most dramatic adventure short of commercial space travel – to create a supersonic airliner.

The sound barrier haunted the 1940s. A few wartime fighter pilots had knocked on its door in vertical dives to find a horrifying world of vibration and stress. After the war came planes which were specifically designed to cross that mystical threshold of 738 mph, the speed at which sound travels through the air. The Americans were first. In 1947 the rocket-driven XS-1, dropped at about 30,000 ft from the belly of a B 29 Superfortress bomber, achieved Mach 1.06 in level flight. The following year Britain's John Derry became the first pilot to break the sound barrier in a conventional jet when he took the swept-wing DH 108 to Mach 1.02 in steep dive from 45,000 ft. The disastrous break-up of Derry's DH 110 at the Farnborough Air Show, killing 30 people as the wreckage scythed through crowds, seemed to underline the enormity of the dangers of supersonic flight. But as pilots were given increasingly sophisticated planes which could achieve supersonic speed in level flight rather than in death-defying nose dives, the terrors began to recede. The growing experience of air force pilots in several countries, notably the USA, Britain and France, showed that transonic flight required intelligent design, not superhuman acts of bravery or even great flying skills.

Planemakers agreed that with the sound barrier beaten, commercial supersonic flight was inevitable and by the mid-1950s several countries were examining the practicalities. Britain set up its Supersonic Transport Advisory Committee in 1956 and invited both Hawker Siddeley and Bristol Aircraft to submit proposals for an SST (supersonic transport). Bristol's creation was delightful, a midwing, slender delta with six turbojets installed in the wings. She would be capable of Mach 2, 1,450 mph, and she fulfilled one of the committee's important requirements, that her technology could be married with a project being carried out in another country. It was already clear that costs would be enormous and that co-operation might be necessary.

Bristol's six-engine design was modified to four – even in the 1950s the designers feared that the sonic boom from six Olympus engines would be unacceptably noisy – and the resemblance to the Super-Caravelle proposed by Sud Aviation of Toulouse in France became all the more striking and all the more propitious. Deals were discussed and on November 29th a formal Anglo-French agreement to develop the plane was signed. The Filton team, now part of the British Aircraft Corporation, and their Sud colleagues set to work. The estimated cost of the work, to be carried out between 1963 and 1970, was put at between £150 and £170 million, to be shared equally by the partner nations.

Concorde might have looked radical, but she wasn't. That delta wing design had a known performance thanks to several very successful military planes, particularly France's supersonic Mirage fighter. Her payload of 132 passengers and design speed of Mach 2 meant she would be built in aluminium, a material aeronautical engineers knew and understood well. The Russians adopted a similar design solution with their Tu-144. It was the Americans who proposed something truly revolutionary with their Boeing 2707, a swing-wing giant which would carry 350 passengers at 1,780 mph and which would require a titanium skin to withstand the higher temperatures of the greater speed.

But if Concorde wasn't radical in design and technology, she would be a novelty in aviation commerce. She was designed to seize the initiative in first class transatlantic travel. With Concorde in service between the capitals of Europe and the United States, no first class passenger would be prepared to cross the Atlantic at subsonic speeds, the argument ran.

In fact Concorde had scant commercial potential beyond the transatlantic route. Her range was little more than the 3,440 mile journey from London to New York. For the really long hauls – to Australia for example – she would need to land and refuel every few hours and then only if the Third World flashing beneath her delta wings was prepared to have the peace of its hills and plains, cities and mountains shattered by big bangs.

On February 20th, 1964 Sir George Edwards, chairman of BAC, made a definitive speech on the technical and commercial background to Concorde. Technically, she was a superb piece of early 1960s engineering which would doubtless achieve the targets set for her. Commercially, he believed, Concorde was bound to succeed. He showed how experience had proved that once an air journey is reduced to less than 12 hours, the volume of passengers rises. He cited the very marked increase in transatlantic travel which had followed the introduction of successful jet airliners, reducing journey time to well under that crucial 12 hour figure.

He continued: 'I am sure that when the New York journey time is down to three hours and the Sydney time down to twelve or thirteen, the traffic and trade figures will have – as, historically, they always have had – a very sharp upward curve'.

He finally turned to the criticism that Britain and France might be better off co-operating on a cheap fare plane for the future. That, he declared, was a red herring. Developing a new airliner with the lowest possible seat mile cost was a separate matter, not an alternative.

While the arguments continued, the engineers at Toulouse and Filton got on with the job. Costs and delays mounted and public Anglo-French concord frequently degenerated into private discord as the two sides bickered, but that was kept quiet. The world outside was fed a rich diet of success stories and those few critics who questioned the wisdom of the project were branded as irresponsible and unpatriotic. The campaign against the 'knockers' conducted by the Bristol press, the *Western Daily Press* in particular, fell little short of vilification. Such blind, jingoistic pro-Concorde fervour was tacitly approved by the politicians.

There was, of course, a very good reason to silence criticism. Britain's entry into the Common Market was increasingly seen not just as desirable but essential, and Concorde became the symbol of Britain's good faith as a European nation. There could be no turning back: Concorde was the price we must pay to win acceptance from a France which had previously barred our entry. Thus the 'knockers' were accused not just of threatening thousands of Bristol jobs and the future of the Bristol aircraft industry, but also of endangering our relations with France and our very future as a successful nation. These were dangerous arguments to bolster an increasingly costly commercial airline venture.

The world's airlines chose to play along with the euphoria and many joined in the fun, cheerfully announcing options on the super-plane of tomorrow. And why not? It cost them nothing and it gave them kudos. The Filton publicity team built a smart display board showing the number of Concorde 'customers' and it looked very impressive . . . Air France, BOAC and Pan American, eight apiece; six each to American Airlines, TWA, United Air Lines and Eastern Air Lines; Air Canada and QANTAS, four; Japan Air Lines, Lufthansa, Continental Airlines and Braniff, three; Middle East Airlines, Air India and Sabena, two. Artists painted pictures of Concordes in the various airline liveries. It added a touch of glamour at a time when air travel was becoming everyday.

But the publicity people couldn't disguise some of Concorde's less attractive features. Some supersonic flights were carried out along western Britain to test public reaction to the sonic boom and there were howls of protest about broken windows and terrified children and animals. Flying supersonic over land, particularly in the western world, clearly wasn't on. An Olympus engine was slung under a bomber and taken for test flights around Filton. The public was aghast at the racket. Soothing press hand-outs reassured the public that these were the silencer-less engines. Once hush kits were installed, noise should provide no problems.

Successive ministers backed Concorde, however great their private misgivings. Only later would Tony Benn, the Bristol MP and Technology Minister of the Harold Wilson government, admit that commercial sanity should have dictated that Concorde be abandoned.

It was far too late. Too much money had been spent, too much national pride invested. There could be no turning back.

The first prototype, 001, was rolled out at Toulouse in December 1967 to begin taxi-ing trials. Bristol's 002 was rolled out from the gigantic Brabazon hanger in September the following year. On Sunday March 2nd, 1969 Sud Aviation's chief test pilot André Turcat took 001 on her maiden flight and, within days, Brian Trubshaw flew 002 from Filton to Fairford in Gloucestershire watched by huge crowds in holiday mood. Both flights were reported and screened around the globe. 'The World Is About To Be Halved' BAC and Sud announced in full page press advertisements. It was Concorde's finest hour.

'Sixteen airlines, seven of them American, have options on 74 Concordes. These airlines handle 60 per cent of free world air travel' chirruped Malcolm Smith, the sunnily optimistic aviation correspondent of the *Bristol Evening Post* in the *Post and Western Daily Press* Maiden Flight Supplement. 'The options will harden into firm orders in 1970 and that's a promising opening to any new chapter of aviation history.' Meanwhile the Russian Tu-144, which had flown well before Concorde and which was due to enter service before long, must not be seen as a threat. Malcolm Smith commented: 'The Russians are not organised on a world basis to give the product support leading airlines demand'.

And as for the Americans? That bold swing-wing design had been abandoned as uneconomic and replaced by a more Concorde-like project which was way behind the Anglo-French development programme. Neither the Americans nor the Russians would offer a challenge, as things turned out. The American designers, chastened by Concorde's bitter experiences in the early and mid-1970s as her fuel hungry, range-limited, noisily anti-social habits attracted increasing distaste from a world becoming more sensitive about its environment, threw in the towel. The Russians fell by the wayside in more tragic circumstances . . . when a Tu-144 exploded in mid-air in front of the world's cameras at the Paris Air Show in 1973. Concordski, as the headline writers called her, did enter service for a while but the project never regained its momentum.

As the Swinging Sixties gave way to the more sober Seventies, Concorde became more and more of an embarrasssment. The oil crisis served to highlight her appetite for fuel – more than twice the fuel per passenger than a conventional airliner – and the environmental lobby her noisiness. Her colossal costs frightened off the airlines and those options fell away as one airline after another decided that the time wasn't right for supersonic travel. Not yet, anyway.

Concorde and her supporters had to fight all the way to get her into service and in the United States, some kindly-disposed authorities had to come up with some very neat footwork – by insisting that permitted noise levels on supersonic aircraft, i.e. Concorde, be judged by different criteria, i.e. noisier – to let her land at all. But she did enter service, thanks to deals between the British and French governments and their national airlines and she is still there, serving British Airways and Air France with their modest but busy fleets of SSTs. The selling line these days is not, if the truth be told, that Corcorde gets you there faster. It is telecommunications, not Concorde, which have halved the world and in the 1980s has come a realisation that arriving a few hours earlier doesn't really make that much difference. You can lose all those hours getting to and from the airport in traffic jams. No, you fly Concorde because she gets you there more smartly. You can cock a snook at the jumbos and airbuses as you soar above them at twice the speed of sound, First Class Travellers of the Stratosphere.

And for those who can't afford the full luxury of the transatlantic dash, there are Concorde 'jollies', pleasure trips to exotic locations like the Pyramids, seats full of well-off trippers or business clients, VIPs and journalists to be flattered with Concorde ties and the rest of the paraphernalia surrounding a flip aboard an SST.

Concorde was a technological triumph and the story of her creation and development still has qualities to inspire the imagination. We must have the courage to fail. But the scale of Concorde's commercial failure – that original estimated cost of £150–£170 million rose to a real figure of more than £1,000 million or £10 for every man, woman and child in Britain – was grotesque. With it went Bristol's chances of developing a successful airliner of its own. And the manner of its failure, to uncritical applause and an unquestioning acceptance of public relations propaganda, has a sinister side. Can we be persuaded so very easily?

One day, perhaps, there will be a new generation of SSTs. A quiet, economic generation of aircraft to speed our children and our children's children across the world in a fraction of the time it takes today but no-one at present is prepared to pursue that dream. Concorde has seen to that.

A. C. H. SMITH
Arts page

In 1960 I was working for the *Evening Post*. I was sent to review a film, *Battle Inferno*. ('Mein Fuehrer, the Sixth Army has collapsed!' 'Don't be sentimental. It was only an army. Set up another one.' They don't write dialogue for Hitler like that any more.) The only other reviewer at the press view was a greasy-haired, loose-lipped lout in a brown suit from the *Evening World*, called Tom Stoppard. We'd never met, and over a glass of sweetish sherry in the Embassy Cinema's office I formed no desire to meet him again. I went back and wrote that the film wasn't much cop, then waited to see what the *World* review would say. Just as I thought: he rated it. Provincial jerk.

Some months later, the Editorial Director of the Bristol United Press, Richard Hawkins, decided to introduce a weekly arts page in the *Western Daily Press*, and invited me to edit it. The bad news was that he asked me to give plenty of work to a local freelance called Stoppard. I sniffed, and rang Stoppard. He said he'd like to kick off with a piece on the New Wave of French film directors. Mon Dieu, I thought to myself, I'll have my work cut out knocking that into shape. When it arrived it was knowledgeable, perceptive, and beautifully written. I didn't change a word. Who *was* this provincial jerk?

We ran the arts page together for nearly three years. I told him that I'd had him down as a greasy-haired lout, and he replied that he'd figured me as a poncey graduate. We agree, nowadays, that our first impressions of each other were not far from the mark. They just left out a bit, like the fact, which we were soon to discover in the course of spending half our lives together in the early '60s, that we both intended to write for a living. I was going to write books, Tom was going to write books, too – he did publish one novel, and some stories – but he also had a yen for the theatre, kindled by his friendship with Peter O'Toole. It was an infectious yen. So was television, later.

At the newspaper, we heard that a chap working upstairs was trying his hand at radio drama. His name was Charles Wood, and his job was to do little drawings for display ads. We got to know him, and his actor pal, Peter Nichols, another would-be playwright, who was doing scripts for television.

In what has always been a private city, with few professional water-holes, the arts page became a focus of sorts for quite a few talented people who were living here, not just passing through (or still at school, like John Cleese). Inevitably, many of the names would not make much of a thud if you dropped them now; but as well as Stoppard, Wood and Nichols, John Arden was here, writing plays while holding a fellowship at the University Drama Department, where Geoffrey Reeves and Michael Kustow arrived as postgraduates and George Brandt was teaching. Until he became a full-time writer, John Hale ran the Bristol Old Vic, where the General Manager was Nat Brenner. Nat and his colleague at the theatre school, Rudi Shelley, are legendary names among the thousands of actors they've taught. At the BBC, Patrick Dromgoole (now boss at HTV West) was Wood's radio drama producer, and John Boorman and Michael Croucher were developing a distinctive school of documentary films. Artists, many of them taught or teaching at the College of Art, included Paul Feiler, Derek Balmer, David Inshaw, Alf Stockham, Neil Murison, Gerry and Anne Hicks, Peter Swan, Geoff Keeling, and Ernie Pascoe. Angela Carter was involved in a brief effort to set up a writers' group. Bristol had its own dance company, Western Theatre Ballet, and its orchestra, the Sinfonia, conducted by Sidney Sager. Even Richard Hawkins' chauffeur at the Bristol United Press, Keith Floyd, has gone on to a different kind of celebrity. Thirty years from now, perhaps someone will be compiling a similar litany of people in Bristol in the late '80s, but I doubt if the list will be a long one. For no reason that I can divine, Bristol and Liverpool both had much more than their share of the country's rich creative surge in the early 1960s. New institutions sprang up in response: the Arts Centre in King Square, which later begat Watershed; and Arnolfini, in the Triangle when it started in 1961.

The social life of writers and actors often led them to Val and Bob Lorraine's house, just behind the Students' Union in Clifton. Stoppard lodged there, at £2 a week, all found. Even then, it was absurdly cheap. Val explained that she wanted to help a young writer in whose talent she had confidence. I wish she'd been able to put a few quid on him at Ladbroke's. I was paying £1.25 a week for a garret flat in Hotwells, where the ceilings were so low that I had to lean over to the left when I played the E string on my fiddle. The derelict house next door was being restored by Martin Shuttleworth, who had succeeded Arden in the drama fellowship. There was no water in Martin's house, so every morning, when he wanted a break, he'd burgle my place by scrambling along a parapet that ran at fourth-floor level the length of the terrace. He'd squeeze in, huge backside first, through the tiny windows of the room where I was usually asleep. 'Thought we could both do with a coffee,' he'd purr.

After that I spent three years in Clifton, at £4 a week, in a flat on top of The Paragon. Stoppard and I saw dawns break in that place planning the arts pages. It had a triangular balcony, commanding a view from Redcliffe to the Suspension Bridge, and overlooked from nowhere except the highest houses in Leigh Woods, across the gorge. I remember 1962 as a fine summer. Britten's *War Requiem* was premièred at Coventry, and I had a recording of it, and lying on my balcony on a hot afternoon, listening to Britten, the girl with me sighed and stretched, and took all her clothes off, to make the most of the sun. I might have said, 'Isn't it a bit early for this? It's only 1962, we haven't got to flower power yet.' What I did say was, 'They could see you from Leigh Woods with binoculars, you know.' 'Let them, if they want it that much,' she answered. I was very impressed. Also, she had a double-barrelled name, and her father made mead. I was starting to get the hang of the 1960s.

Geoffrey Reeves was ruthless in exploiting his friends, in return for massive meals, and it was on one of my days as his taxi-driver that I met Alison Kennedy, a drama student. We got married in 1963, with Tom as my best man, and she moved into The Paragon. It might have been the prospect of filming the view from our balcony which put into John Boorman's mind the notion of using us as his 'eyes' for a documentary series about Bristol.

I'd already worked once with Boorman. He was making a studio programme about Arnold Wesker's Centre 42 Crusade to disseminate the arts through the trades unions, saw some stuff about Wesker by me in the arts page (both Reeves and Kustow were working for Wesker), asked me to go and see him at the BBC, and when we met told me that I was going to front the programme, for 60 minutes on BBC-1 nationwide, live. I told him that not only had I never looked a tv camera in the eye, but I didn't even have a tv set at home. 'Good,' he said, 'you won't be burdened by preconceptions.' There was no autocue then. The script I wrote was copied onto idiot boards, large capital letters held beside the camera by a PA. Half-way through addressing the nation, I found myself being offered words which, even in my condition of catatonic fear, I recognised as having nothing to do with what I was supposed to be on about. The PA had got the boards in the wrong order. I suppose that's why they were called idiot boards, they were operated by an idiot. I ad-libbed my way somehow to the next item, and am glad, now, that there was no video then. I wouldn't want to join the millions watching me go through that. I've done hundreds of tv programmes since then, but nothing – not totally dried

41

interviewees, nor totally wet and unstoppable ones, not even a craned camera slowly collapsing like a giraffe with a broken neck – could ever match that first gut feeling.

Boorman's new series was called *The Newcomers*, and was part of the launch of BBC-2 in 1964. I was supposed to script it, but instead got cast as a character, in search of Bristol. At seven months pregnant, and with four of the six films already in the can, Alison was told it was going to be twins. Hold the front page! The series was already news – Boorman pioneered documentaries on ordinary lives, but the tabloids saw it differently, since anyone appearing on television became a celebrity thereby. When word got out that it was going to be twins, photographers were climbing through the windows of The Paragon. Our landlady, Ruth Stephenson, got rid of them by using her skills as a former actress. She picked up her dog, Jessie, unmuzzled her and threw her at the *Daily Express*, while shrieking, 'My god, she hasn't got her muzzle on!'

Boorman wanted to shoot a sequence in a swish flat, and asked me if I knew one. I took him round to meet Richard Hawkins. Sitting us down in his palatially spartan drawing-room, Richard offered us a drink, from the many bottles beside the fireplace. Boorman and I each consented to a whisky. Talking away, Richard poured me a glass of the single malt he knew I liked, corked the bottle, uncorked a bottle of cooking whisky, and gave Boorman a glass of that. The film-maker was much too inquisitive not to ask, 'Tell me, Richard, why did you give Anthony one kind of whisky and me another kind?' Richard realised what, absent-mindedly, he'd done, and could see no way out of it except by telling the truth. 'Well, you look like the kind of man who'd put water in his whisky.' Boorman used to tell that story with delight.

Stoppard and Balmer also featured in *The Newcomers*, and most of our friends had bit-parts; Martin Shuttleworth used his appearance to show off his best party small-talk – 'I always say that history is the black sheep uncle whose debts I repudiate.' But the star, as Boorman intended, was the city of Bristol. Watching it now, you remember how seductively seedy Clifton was: peeling grandeur, prams and bikes in the corniced halls, lots of real shops, grocers, ironmongers, Mr Neshitch the tailor, Kirby's for ham and Cheddar, and just two cars parked in Cornwallis Crescent. Peter Hawkins wrote a song about the place:

> A pile of Georgian jerry-building high up on a hill,
> Left to genteel sherry-drinking ladies in a will,
> Inhabited by hairy-heads who rarely pay their bills,
> And property-developers clo-osing for the kill . . .

Yes the kill.

When my daughters were born, and we were looking for a family home where we didn't have to lug carry-cots up 81 stairs, Charles Wood, living in Redland, said, 'Come on over this side of Whiteladies Road. It's lovely here, and cheaper.' We did move to Redland, into the house where I still am. Charles moved to Clifton three weeks later.

In 1964, a lot of us gathered at Boorman's house, in Cotham, to watch the General Election comprehensively covered by tv. While the results were declared, and plotted by Robert McKenzie's cardboard arrow known as the Swingometer, the sort of toy you wouldn't hope to get in a packet of cereals, most of us, on Boorman's whim, were playing chess. I remember beating Boorman's co-director Michael Croucher with a reckless king-side pawn blitz. Stoppard likes chess, but he was no grandmaster. Nor was I, but I always used to beat him. Once, when I moved a piece and announced 'Check mate', Stoppard looked ruefully at me, not the board and murmured, 'Every time I allow this to happen I feel I should apologise for having interrupted your train of thought.' At ping-pong, he used to beat me. We'd always get to deuce, then he'd win. Maybe he was quite a bit better than I was, but discreet.

At Boorman's house we cheered, in 1964, as thirteen years of Tory rule came to an end, just. I'd canvassed for Labour. In 1966, after eighteen months of Wilson, I didn't even vote. At meetings of Tony Benn's New Bristol Group, in Victoria Street, I'd imagined something else when Labour came to power.

What I had imagined seemed at last to be happening in 1968 – in Paris, for sure, in Prague perhaps, in Vietnam at a terrible cost, and very hesitantly in Britain. What I imagined in the early sixties is what I still imagine now, living in Stalag Thatcher. As far as I'm concerned, the 1960s have never ended: what's been going on for 20 years is a dreadful music and frozen caption while we wait for normal service to be resumed. I'm not nostalgic for the sixties. I leave that to those who were born in them, who are attracted by the fashions of those times but know little of the feelings that authentically produced student sit-ins, hippies, flowered ties, Pink Floyd, and the wonderful rest of it. It was a feeling of freedom, of social, if not political, revolution. The old order – what D. H. Lawrence called 'the grey ones' – had been discredited, by mockery. Peter Cook, *Private Eye*, *That Was The Week That Was*, the Profumo affair, *Catch-22* – all of them, and the list could go on and on, served above all to rouse a spirit of irreverence, of refusal to be bowed-down by hallowed pieties and conventions. We were going to inherit the earth, but we were not going about it meekly.

I can pinpoint what was, for me, the crucial moment of the 1960s. I have no idea where I was when I heard they'd shot President Kennedy, but I know just where I was sitting in the Arts Centre on April 28th, 1967, to watch Charles Wood's *Dingo*, banned from public theatres by the Lord Chamberlain and so performed under a club licence, in a boxing-ring set, directed by Geoffrey Reeves. In North Africa a soldier in a tank has, to quote the stage directions, 'been burned to death in a sitting position. He is black; charred, thin as a black, dried-in-the-sun, long dead bean. His arms are bent over his pin-head to open his hatch. Bits of still intact khaki drill flap from the crook of his elbows, crutch, and round his ankles.' Tom Kempinski, playing Dingo with a weary, foul tongue and infinitely compassionate eye, stared at the remains:

> . . . it's not Chalky. Do you think we'd make a mistake like that? Do you think that black, burnt up, high in the sun stinking charred old toothy old jerk of raw material is a British swaddie do you? Do you think we'd risk offending evey mother here tonight with unlikely looking material. Highly upset they'd be. That's enemy. People out there lost their dear ones – that's enemy. No British soldier dies like that. That's enemy. You won't find a photograph, a statue, a painting of a British soldier like that.

That it was twenty years before the man who wrote *Dingo* became nationally known, for *Tumbledown*, is one of the bad jokes that writers tell each other between arguments about who's got the most macho overdraft and whose agent is the biggest wimp. After they'd had plays on in London, Wood and Nichols were each treated by the Bristol Old Vic to one week's run of a play, at the Little Theatre, both filling about 30 per cent of the seats. Wood's *Cockade* took another swipe at military myths, and blew up a storm in the local papers. One chap wrote to ask why we had to put up with stuff like this when there were perfectly 'wholesome' plays begging to be done. As example, he cited *King Lear*. At least Wood and Nichols got a week each. Stoppard fared less well. He offered the Old Vic the world première of a play called *Rosencrantz & Guildenstern Are Dead*, but they said it did not fit in with their production requirements. (On the arts page, Tom and I had flirted with a more honest form of rejection slip: The Editor thanks you for your contribution, but deeply regrets that it is a load of crap.)

And so they moved away, inevitably in the direction of London, first Stoppard, then Nichols ('I've run out of places in Bristol to take my kids to on Sunday'), and finally Wood. It's idle, and naive, to speculate what Bristol might be now if it had cared to cherish talents like theirs. Civically, the city always has been small-minded. Meanwhile, the arts page was decimated, 'for commercial reasons', which was odd since the circulation put on 2,000 every Monday, arts page day. I never did understand accountancy. The truth was that the page was personally destroyed by an editor who hated what he thought was all arty piffle.

Only some of it was arty piffle. It had its unpiffling moments. One of them had been a campaign that Stoppard and I ran for a Bristol Arts Trust to be formed. Overnight, committees of businessmen, academics and trades unionists formed themselves to support the idea. The City Council adopted it as an unopposed Lord Mayor's motion, and then contrived to bury it with no funeral or public inquest. Now, nearly 30 years later, the City Council has come up with a proposal to form a Bristol Arts Trust.

Boorman left the BBC to make his first feature film, *Catch Us If You Can*. Featuring the Dave Clark Five, it was a feeble imitation of *Help!*, which Wood had scripted for the Beatles. Boorman got Nichols to script his film. Peter was soon in despair, as he discovered what I'd already experienced, that to Boorman a script is nothing more than a plausible excuse to take his crew to a location, where he makes up the film as he goes along. Sensibly, he scripts his own films now.

I was cast as a beach photographer in *Catch Us If You Can*, and was called upon to have sand kicked in my face by Dave Clark himself, a piece of acting which he was able to accomplish by not attempting to chew gum at the same time. Boorman's next film, made in Hollywood, was *Point Blank*. After *Catch Us*, it was as though the bloke who took 1–70 against Nempnett Thrubwell 2nd XI last week had bowled out the West Indians at Lord's.

Boorman lives in Eire now. Nichols is in Shropshire, writing plays about why he'll never write another play. Wood is in Oxfordshire; I worked with him a few years ago, novelizing his screenplay of *Wagner*. Reeves directed Wood's *H* at the National, worked for the RSC, and ran theatres in Exeter and Nottingham. We spent the summer of 1971 together in Iran, with Peter Brook's company, and an autumn recently in Atlanta, doing a production of *Pericles*. Kustow went to the RSC, where I followed him, then to the ICA, the National, before becoming Channel 4's Commissioning Editor for arts programmes. Richard Hawkins is still on the board of the BUP, but lives in France, surrounded by more animals than Dr Dolittle. Derek Balmer remains in Bristol, doing so well at photography that he paints just for kicks. I kick him. Stoppard lives near Slough. I once collaborated with him on a screenplay, but the combination wasn't as successful as the one I unwittingly initiated by introducing him to a Keynsham doctor called Miriam who had approached Alison and me after seeing *The Newcomers*.

All the time, the grey ones have been closing for the kill. Don't be sentimental. It was only an extraordinary half-decade in Bristol. Set up another one.

JAMES BELSEY

Radical Chic and Rock 'n' Roll

'You,' said the girl in a startlingly emotionless voice, 'are the lackey of the fascist capitalist press'. She may even have used the expression 'lickspittle lackey' but it was all a long time ago and I can't be sure. I was nothing of the sort, of course. I was merely a young hack from the *Bristol Evening Post*. Part of me was the paper's rock writer or Pop Correspondent as we were primly known as a breed in the 1960s, most of me was a rather lowly news reporter and the tiny, remaining portion of me was the paper's University Correspondent. She was a member of the Praetorian guard defending the entrance to Bristol University's Senate House. This was the winter which had followed the Spring of 68.

There are lots and lots of 1960s. There was the Sixties of Adam Faith and Eden Kane, trained puppets of the emerging pop circuit who, despite their neat John Michael suits and slim, horizontal striped ties, hadn't altogether lost the soul of the old music hall and whose pretty little tributes to Someone Else's Baby owed far more to the traditions of Tin Pan Alley than to the brooding south of Mississippi which bred Elvis and all that followed him. There was the 60s of the Beatles and the Mersey Beat which took the story a little further. There was the chic 60s of Mary Quant and the King's Road with its down-market imitators and progeny in Carnaby Street and an emerging breed of British musicians with a liberal, often art school, education.

And then came the moment that proved a watershed, when radical became chic once more. If I had to select a date when all that had passed as fab and gear or grotty suddenly appeared faded and old hat while words like didactic and eclectic, radical, nay revolutionary seemed newly-minted and when Trotsky and Marcuse, Guevara and even Lenin replaced a more frivolous pantheon of heroes like Jagger and Lennon, I would choose June 25th, 1967. The event was a BBC-TV spectacular hosted by Cliff Michelmore which broadcast blurry but live pictures from across the globe and, as a climax and the chief British contribution to this momentous episode in broadcasting history, the avuncular Michelmore introduced the Beatles recording 'All You Need Is Love' from the Abbey Road studios. It was a moment of the deepest embarrassment. The Beatles and their fab friends, the Stones among them, had gathered together to celebrate themselves and they wore all the airs and graces – and silly clothes – of a new aristocracy. It was a fatal mistake. We, the punters, did not want a new aristocracy. The Beatles' impertinent arrogance had been distorted into smugness. They had become theirs, no longer ours and the appearance did untold damage to the credibility of the Sgt Pepper album which had been released on June 1st. To make matters worse, the sheer momentum of the Beatles' career ensured enough sales for 'All You Need Is Love' to reach Number One on July 19th, a position it took from Procol Harum's 'A Whiter Shade of Pale'. But the Beatles got their just deserts. Their hit was replaced by the dotty ditty 'San Francisco' (Be Sure To Wear Some Flowers In Your Hair).

I coveted two positions when I joined the *Evening Post* in the summer of 1966. I wanted to write about pop music because I couldn't begin to afford all the records I craved, let alone the pop shows (*not* concerts in those days . . . half a dozen three-minute songs was the limit even for the head-line acts) at the Colston Hall. And I wanted to write about students because we lived in raffish heart of Clifton, in a basement on West Mall, and you couldn't get to the bars of the few decent pubs in what the estate agents now call Clifton Village without barging your way through as interesting a group of young people as you'd find anywhere. I was 22 and I quickly got both jobs. Michael Green, our pop writer, left for London where he would eventually become an ageless TV reporter and the university job turned out to be vacant. So the free records began pouring in and when I wasn't playing music I was cultivating student contacts at the brand new students' union in Queen's Road and writing stories about them.

Polite stories, for the most part, because Bristol University students were a polite lot. The student president was an upright, public school sort of chap who knew how to behave himself at sherry parties with the Vice-Chancellor and he had his elected consort, the Lady President, the official hostess and dispenser of charm school smiles. She was Sue Lawley who – it was generally acknowledged – was, well, gracious.

Radical had been chic right at the very start of the Sixties, as those of us who trod that cheerful path from Aldermaston to London in the wake of such Pied Pipers as Canon Collins and Michael Foot can testify. The four days of the march was an education in radical politics – you discovered that communists didn't actually have horns on their heads and anarchists didn't all wear long black cloaks, wide-brimmed hats and carry black spheres marked Bomb. But the mood passed and with it went the duffle-coat, trad jazz and all that ban-the-bombing. Young consumerism triumphed, clinging to the coat-tails of the great spenders themselves, the Fab Four.

47

By 1967 protest was returned to favour and an initially dumbfounded student population in Bristol was abuzz with talk of the sight of its Lady President, a flower or two in her hitherto perfectly arranged hair, walking hand-in-hand down the streets of Clifton with one of the most ferociously articulate radicals among the undergraduates, one Big Mac. He was well over six foot tall and had flaming red hair. It was as if the Lady President had given her personal benediction to the return of the radical movement among the young.

The music was changing too, and away from commercial cuteness. The turn of 1967 into 1968 saw Cream in the charts with 'I Feel Free' and the astonishing arrival of the Jimi Hendrix Experience with 'Hey Joe', all within a few weeks that December and January. Hendrix arrived in Bristol on one of those jam-packed roadshows they used to send round Britain. He came on stage immediately after a brief appearance by Engelbert Humperdinck and played three ear-shattering numbers. Bizarre barely describes the culture clash between 'Please Release Me' and 'Purple Haze', but there it was. Cream came too, but their domain was the students' union in Clifton. The bluesier bands tended to stick to the student circuit and Saturday nights at the union saw many heroes. Fleetwood Mac were regulars and I had to buy both Mick Fleetwood and John McVie beers because they were too broke to buy their own, and we saw Chicken Shack and Julie Driscoll, the Move (who smashed up a TV set on stage shouting 'Freak Out') and the smarter Bristol bands like the Franklin Big Six.

The silly, sappy summer of love of 67 meant lots of flower power and, naturally, lots of silly headlines in the local press. The Bristol Flower Show was a headline writer's dream that year. A subterranean drug culture developed, mostly based on cannabis but with a minority who experimented with the flavour of the year acid, or LSD. Acid trips usually frightened the wits out of those who braved them and, anyway, there were headier thrills than chemical-induced ecstasy and fear. There were student politics, and the movement was world-wide. It began, awkwardly, with Flower Power in San Franciso, an attempt to pretend that the Vietnam war wasn't happening and it gathered momentum with startling rapidity. The college campus became a hotbed of noisy protest and it spread across the United States and leapt the Atlantic with barely a flicker.

By the spring of 68 Bristol's brightest young radicals, who would have counted themselves lucky to have attracted an audience of more than a couple of dozen of their chums at political meetings, found themselves performing before hundreds. Revolution was the flavour of the year, however skin-deep it might have been. Where have all the Ché Guevara posters gone?

Representatives of the North Vietnamese locked in that bitter, tragic struggle with the United States, came down to the students' union to spread the word and when the students of Paris seemed to threaten a real revolution, it wasn't long before some of their leading characters turned up in Bristol. By summer, with exams safely out of the way, Bristol University's students and some more radical staff declared a Free University at the students' union, made long and impassioned speeches and, one weekend, declared that they were occupying the building! No matter that it was theirs in the first place. Some right-minded (literally) sparks lobbed a small petrol bomb at the building from a passing car but the flames, like the sit-in, flickered away harmlessly.

'The cause is not the cause' was the cry and for the great majority of the young, that was true. But among their number were some true radicals with a cold-hearted, dogmatic vision of a ruthlessly egalitarian society which would allow no deviation from their beliefs and their visions. And this was their hour in Bristol.

For, in the autumn of 68, they found the Cause. It irked the radicals that they, as undergraduates, were children of privilege and the symbol of their privilege was the union building. It was a far cry from the shabby students' unions you found at the College of Commerce in Unity Street and across at Bristol Technical College on Ashley Down. What is ours must be yours, and the university students passed a resolution declaring that all students of further education in Bristol would henceforth be offered reciprocal membership at the Queen's Road building. Bristol University's authorities, hopelessly at odds with the mood of the times, forbade it. The radicals hardly dared to believe their luck! What a cause! Even the *Evening Post* was moved to write a stern editorial criticising the university for its shameless élitism.

And so the plot was hatched. The radical leaders held a clandestine meeting to sort out their tactics. They chose to organise a march on Senate House, the university's administrative headquarters, which would swiftly orchestrate into an occupation of the building. They would close the university down until its authorities capitulated over reciprocal membership and once *that* victory had been achieved they would turn their attention to the wider business of creating an egalitarian university and once *that* victory was theirs, they would turn their attention to the big world outside to sort its inequalities and wrong-headedness.

They achieved the first, the seizure of Senate House, with an ease that surprised even them. The university's staff were refused admission, a state-within-a-state was declared with revolutionary committees, revolutionary rules and endless revolutionary meetings, electric with atmosphere, charged with emotion. The passion was so

49

exacting, so lofty that there are still people 20 years later who've never quite come down from that brilliant high they experienced in the days of December 1968. An orange-red flag was raised over the building and forays of reactionaries (the rugby-playing, scrag 'em engineers to the fore) and, of course, the fascist capitalist press were quickly seen off by the Praetorian guard entrusted with keeping enemies at bay. Statements were issued, some media invited to inspect the sit-in – but no cameras . . . they weren't *that* revolutionary and didn't want mummy and daddy recognising them on the telly – and endless, long-winded leaflets were written and distributed. 'The language is pure Marxist' one dazed professor told me as he read one of them.

The sit-in staggered on for twelve days. It was the longest university sit-in in Britain. It ended when the whiff of roast turkey and the sound of popping corks back in the hundreds of largely middle-class homes from which the young people had come became too strong. It all ended in some minor legal action, tedious disciplinary hearings and a loss of nerve among the university's old guard. Most of the radical leaders were in their final year and there were degrees to get. The world had moved on.

Three Days Of Peace and Music came to Woodstock in the summer of 69 and that suddenly seemed a much more attractive way of changing the world than occupying dull, bureaucratic buildings and the huge event brought a sigh of contentment you could even hear in Bristol that summer. What we hadn't known was that that sigh was, in reality, a final gasp.

Everyone who was young mourned the passing of the decade and desperately sought to re-enact its best moments. In the summer of 1970 the Bath Festival spilled over into a gigantic rock and pop festival of Woodstock proportions when some 400,000 young people made the pilgrimage to the Bath and West Show ground at Shepton Mallet to listen to some of the then greatest rock bands in the world. I spent two dizzy days in the backstage village, meeting heroes in every corner, including one afternoon with Roger McGuinn of the Byrds, whose jingle-jangle music still conjures up the 60s more vividly than any others.

I interviewed other men and women with long, long hair and tie-and-dye T-shirts. One wore a jacket of faded purple velvet, and his hair fell over his shoulders. He was a bank clerk from Middlesex and a hippy at the weekends.

When Led Zeppelin came on stage at the crescendo of this monumental event, some people lit a bonfire and danced frenziedly around it. A fire engine somehow found a path through the hundreds of thousands of writhing bodies and put out the flames. It was a superfluous gesture . . . the fire of the Sixties was out already.

MARY ACKLAND
The Berni revolution

Back in the 1950s, before the age of Berni really began, you had to know the rules if you went for a meal in a restaurant. They were subtle, complex and daunting, perfectly designed to keep outsiders at arms' length. The diner needed the correct clothes, the right background and a breezy self-confidence which asserted that he or she had a perfect right to be there, commanding respect from the waiters. Fail the tests and be intimidated by lengthy menus written in obscure French, a wine list that was incomprehensible in its detail and, of course, by a staff who could turn civility into superciliousness at the hint of the wrong gesture.

Frank and Aldo Berni knew that. But, unlike so many of their contemporaries in the restaurant business, they yearned for a great mass of customers, not the cosy exclusivity of a charmed circle of upper-class diners. The brothers grew up in a catering family. Their grandmother and father had run temperance bars, fashionable in late Victorian and Edwardian England, selling soft drinks, sweets, ice cream, coffee and tobacco. The business was ruined by the First World War but in 1931, when they were left £150 each by their mother, the brothers opened their own restaurant in High Street, Exeter. They went on to buy Hort's restaurant in Broad Street, Bristol and soldiered on through the Second World War and rationing, buoyed up by their conviction that once austerity and rationing came to an end, they would prosper.

Between the smart, exclusive restaurant with its (usually) fancy French food, the Corner House and the fish-and-chip shop, there was a yawning gap. The Bernis hoped to exploit it. Meat rationing ended in 1954 and, the following year, the brothers bought the Rummer in St Nicholas Market, Bristol. Their moment had come. The Rummer is a rabbit warren of a place with cellar bars and rooms large and small as well as a history as an inn which dates back to the 13th century. They called in a clever designer, Alex Waugh, who created several restaurants and bars under one roof and cultivated an olde worlde, lived-in, almost shabby look. No-one need feel out of place in this atmosphere! Alex Waugh made a famous remark to the Bernis when he arrived. 'If you've got cobwebs, keep 'em. If you haven't, I'll make you some!' Now that was *very* clever for 1955.

But if appearance was important, the choice of good food, or rather, lack of choice, was crucial. Frank Berni had visited the United States and been struck by the huge success of the all-American steak bar with its carefully-controlled portions, its strictly limited menus and its almost obsessive quality control. You could eat a steak meal on the East Coast, drive 3,000 miles to California and then order an identical meal at an identical establishment. The English, freed of meat rationing at last, wanted steaks . . . 'and we decided to give it to them,' Frank said.

The brothers planned down to the last detail. They were determined that every last worry about eating-out would be removed, making Berni catering attractive to the mass market. The fixed-price, limited item menu ensured that customers knew exactly how much they would be paying. The wine list was cut to just 16 names, eight red, six white and two rosé. One innovation was the marketing of sherry to go with the meal. This was sold from the wood in large schooners. The Bernis had observed one of England's more curious social traits, that the drinking of sherry was considered both respectable and harmless. No matter that two or three large schooners was the equivalent of a modest binge. After all, bishops and maiden aunts approved . . .

The Rummer was the prototype. The revolution quickly followed. The Berni brothers discovered by trial, and remarkably few errors, how to run a successful multiple restaurant under one roof. By ringing the changes from room to room, they were able to encourage their loyal and growing following to come back time and again. The visitor would find Steak and Duck in one room, Chicken and Ham in a second, possibly Steak and Plaice in a third, all cooked in full view of the diners, a ploy which added to the lively atmosphere. There were never more than four complete dinners on the menu in any room and there were no complications with à la carte extras. There weren't any! By 1968, the empire firmly established, joint managing director Mr. C.M. Cockerill, could proclaim: 'In effect, we've told the public what to eat and what to drink. The very fact that they don't have much of a choice is our drawing card'!

He could point to all the tangible symbols of success. A Berni Inns logo that was recognised throughout Britain. A national chain of 98 Berni Inns with 230 individual restaurants and 460 bars. A system of quality and quantity control that was famous for its precision. There were jokes about how Bernis managed to come up with 8 million identical-sized steaks in a year but they did and that reliability was an invaluable asset.

A typical late 60s Berni menu tells as much about the Sixties as any Beatles record. Here's one from the Steak Bar at a Berni:

Prime Fillet Steak, 15s 6d (77p); Prime Rump Steak, 12s 9d (63p); Prime Sirloin Steak, 12s 3d (61p), all the steaks half pound approximate weight, and all 'Grilled to your liking and served with button mushrooms, tomato, watercress, chipped potatoes, roll and butter and, to follow, ice cream or a choice of cheese and biscuits'. Or, as the alternative, Golden Fried Fillet of Plaice, 8s (40p), 7 ounces approximate uncooked weight 'served with tartare sauce, lemon, watercress, chipped potatoes, roll and butter and, to follow, Ice Cream or a choice of cheese and biscuits'.

That same menu has a wine list by then expanded to 18 wines, eight red, eight white and two rosé, ranging in price from Champagne at £2 2s 6d (£2 12p) and a Burgundy, Nuits St Georges at 26s 6d (£1 32p) to a Spanish Sauternes at 13s 6d (67p).

Thanks to the Bernis the English discovered the pleasures of eating out – something the Europeans had always taken for granted. The brothers had opened up a mass market and towards the end of the decade a young generation of entrepreneurial restaurateurs was anxious to exploit it. A bare two miles from The Rummer, Keith Floyd was perfecting the concept of the British bistro . . . but that's another story.

MARY ACKLAND

Arnolfini: the honeymoon years

From the very beginning there was nothing quite like the Arnolfini.
Its style was unmistakable . . . cool clear open space with clever diffuse
lighting which cunningly illuminated what mattered most – the big
bold paintings on the gallery walls.

Of course there was modern art in Bristol before the Arnolfini.
However, contemporary, progressive painting and sculpture was still
being displayed in traditional surroundings. The Arnolfini offered no
compromises – it existed solely for the purpose of showing the very
latest and best modern work in the right surroundings.

Jeremy Rees spent five years dreaming up his gallery and another 25
running it. He saw it through its beginning in the early 1960s, directed
it through its expansion and international successes in the 1970s and
early 1980s and shouldered its burdens as a financial crisis deepened in
the mid-1980s, an era far less indulgent towards the arts than the daring
1960s had been. He left the Arnolfini sadly, unsure whether it might
not have been better to start all over again: to, perhaps, attempt to
recapture the original, optimistic spirit of that first gallery. . . But too
much had happened and he left with reassurances (albeit belated) from
every side that here in Bristol he had created something very special
indeed.

Today, Bristol has more than a dozen well-established, active
galleries at work alongside the larger institutions like the City Art
Gallery, the Royal West of England Academy, the Watershed media
centre and, of course, the Arnolfini itself. It would take a conscientious
visitor a couple of days to do justice to all the exhibitions on show at
any one time. The Bristol Jeremy Rees first knew barely had a glimpse
of contemporary art. Neither, mind you, did the rest of provincial
England.

Jeremy Rees arrived in Bristol in 1953 as a management trainee with
the print company of Allen Davies. In Bristol there were only two
places to see painting and sculpture: the Royal West of England
Academy with its very traditional shows and the City Art Gallery
which, besides its permanent displays, staged the occasional touring
exhibitions, often, predictably, from the Victoria and Albert Museum
in London.

Jeremy Rees' firm sent him for a three-year course at the London College of Printing. While in London he met and married his wife, Annabel, and discovered a lasting fascination with print and design. He also came across the Institute of Contemporary Art, then a little first-floor gallery in Dover Street. The ICA introduced him to a young generation of British artists, Denny, Richard Hamilton and Eduardo Paolozzi among them, and he became determined to show the excitement of this work in Bristol. If there wasn't the equivalent of an ICA in Bristol by the time he got back, he'd have a go at creating one.

These idealistic ambitions were held at bay by National Service. He spent a year kicking his heels in Sierra Leone and as there wasn't much else to do tried to sort out his own ideas about his future and his gallery. When Jeremy Rees returned to Bristol there was still nothing remotely like the ICA but a new generation of British artists were waiting in the wings. The excitement and innovation of the Sixties was clearly shown in British painting and sculpture.

Jeremy Rees already knew the sort of artists he wanted to introduce to Bristol. But, to set up his gallery he needed money, premises and a name. He consulted his parents (his mother, Jean Rees, is a well-known West Country painter) who had helped set up the Bridgwater Arts Centre, and Cyril Wood, who co-ordinated the Arts Council's efforts in the South West.

Jeremy and Annabel Rees put in £100 each and John and Jenny Orsborn, whom they'd met through Bristol painter Peter Swan, put up a third £100. They found premises in a roomy first floor area in Triangle West, Clifton, strategically placed midway between those established bastions of the arts, the City Art Gallery and the Royal West of England Academy. And then the name. They wanted something unusual, even enigmatic, and memorable. They tried several, including the Unicorn after Bristol's heraldic symbol. Then Jeremy Rees remembered a private publisher named Jan Arnolfini whose nuptials were the subject of Van Eyck's masterpiece, *The Marriage of the Arnolfini*. The painting hangs in the National Gallery. And, Bristol got a name that tantalized and a gallery it couldn't ignore.

With his strong interest in design, Jeremy Rees was determined to create a house style at the Arnolfini down to the smallest detail: even the light bulbs mattered. Everything must relate to the new spirit, even enhance it: the decor, the lettering on the gallery directions and notepaper, the letterhead logo, functional but elegant furniture. The place might not be overpopulated with staff but the few present were always prepared to listen, help or explain. And, always, a good stock of prints and reading material. Here was an ambiance and look new to

Bristol but which over the years became an accepted statement of artistic appreciation – as many Arnolfini prints and calendars have been pinned up or framed as Aubrey Beardsleys and Pirellis – in the right circles of course!

The choice of artists for the very first exhibition clarified intentions and set the standard. All work must be by living artists. And, good art speaks for itself. So, there was work on paper by the Polish artist Josef Herman and paintings by the young Bristol artist Peter Swan. It was the characteristic Arnolfini blend of a young, innovative West Country painter being shown alongside an international reputation.

Those first hand-to-mouth days were exhilarating. Jeremy and Annabel took turns with the Orsborns to staff the gallery. It wasn't long before the Arnolfini began to make friends in a city where Jeremy, from Bridgwater, and Annabel, from London, knew very few people. Hans Schubart, director of the City Art Gallery, was encouraging. Anne Hewer, so closely involved with the arts in Bristol, was an early ally. Word spread further and some of London's modern art galleries, including Kasmin's and Waddington's, made contact as well as new galleries in several other provincial cities which were following a similar path to the Arnolfini. Joint touring exhibitions with financial burdens being shared became an exciting venture. Print-making was attracting a new generation of artists and this resurgence was shown at the Arnolfini through displays and in a comprehensive collection of prints for sale by artists like David Hockney and Roy Lichtenstein. A most unusual feature at the gallery was the permanent exhibition of contemporary jewellery by artists such as Gerda Flockinger, reflecting the Rees' interest in the art.

The exhibitions attracted good audiences. Triangle West, Clifton is in the Bristol University area and it was only a matter of time before teachers and students from the University and local art colleges became regular visitors. School teachers brought their sixth form art groups. There was critical recognition, locally and nationally. Even sales of paintings and prints went well. But, the Arnolfini had no solid financial base. Annabel's parents came to the rescue on more than one occasion when the gallery desperately needed a few hundred pounds to tide it over. In 1965, with three artistically successful but financially tricky years behind it, the Arnolfini became an educational charity. It received its first public funding in donations from the Gulbenkian Foundation to carry out repairs on the unsatisfactory roof. The Arts Council provided an annual grant of £1,500 with a further £350 from the Bristol City Council to help the Arnolfini carry on its work as a gallery. On Anne Hewer's advice, the gallery's friends were invited to buy shares which raised a few thousand pounds. Then, Peter Barker-

Mill, an artist and designer, set up a trust for the Arnolfini which ensured some future financial stability.

The excitement of the exhibitions seemed to generate a continuing momentum. Over the years shows featured the St. Ives group, Bridget Riley's Op Art, Anthony Caro's sculpture to the emergence of a new romanticism in the pre-Ruralist work of David Inshaw. But the Arnolfini was now attempting to display art both visual and performed under its roof. There were screenings of avant garde continental films as an antidote to the commercial fare on offer in local cinemas. American Beat poet Alan Ginsberg was a guest during a poetry event. And, who can forget that wildly ambitious open air sculpture exhibition throughout Bristol in which, miraculously, the pieces were left unscathed! As the 1960s ended the Arnolfini seemed to be leading a charmed life. Its reputation was by now international and its innovations, including pioneering the business sponsorship of the arts, admired and imitated not just by British arts groups but also their European counterparts.

The gallery at Triangle West was bursting at the seams. Jeremy Rees longed to start a cinema and stage music and dance events on a regular basis. There should be a lively, well-stocked shop for prints, books, records. And, why shouldn't visitors and audiences be able to eat and drink at the Arnolfini as well? It was time to move.

In 1970, the Arnolfini set up in larger premises in a disused Queen Square warehouse. This was meant to be a temporary move before creating a purpose built centre on Castle Park by Bristol Bridge. This did not happen, so the gallery and its expanding staff made yet another temporary encampment at W Shed in Canons Road, later to become the home of Watershed. Meanwhile, building work went on at Bush House across St. Augustine Reach which the Arnolfini would share with the JT Group. In 1975 Bush House was ready and the Arnolfini could now offer dance and music programmes, films and books, a video library, a restaurant and wine bar, galleries large enough for three sizeable exhibitions at a time, workshops for adults and children.

The move was significant in many ways. It not only gave Bristol an arts organization that was the envy of other provincial cities, it also pioneered the revitalization of Bristol's derelict docklands. However, the reaction of Bristol's city councillors, with a few notable exceptions – including Bob, now Sir Robert Wall – was of indifference if not hostility. It mattered not a whit that Jeremy Rees could point out that hundreds of thousands of people visited the Arnolfini, that it had made such an enormous contribution educationally, communally and artistically to the city, that the change of fortunes in dockside Bristol had been initiated by the Arnolfini. The City Council ignored the increasingly desperate pleas for help as money troubles multiplied in the 1980s. The Arts Council's new policy of insisting that local authorities match Arts Council grants brought despair. Jeremy Rees seriously considered closing the Bush House centre and re-trenching in smaller premises – perhaps, a return to the gallery-only days of the 1960s . . . The summer of 1987 forced the painful realisation by the board of the Arnolfini and Jeremy Rees himself that a price had to be paid. Programmes were drastically reduced, an accountancy exercise slimmed the finances and Jeremy Rees was out. But not abandoned by the arts world. His enormous experience makes him a valued consultant not just in this country but abroad and he and Annabel have moved to London.

Jeremy Rees left the Arnolfini with many regrets but only one tinged with bitterness, that the Arnolfini's contribution to the life of Bristol had been so shabbily treated by Bristol City Council. 'That really did depress me and upset me, particularly towards the end of my time there. It was unfair'.

But, in his characteristically fair-minded and optimistic way, Jeremy Rees adds 'I never minded the rude remarks when we put on controversial exhibitions – and we had plenty of those. It didn't bother me in the least that some people called us the Arnol-phoney. I thought that was quite funny, actually. Just as long as people came and made up their minds. Which so many people did do. And, I'm glad to see, still do'.

JEREMY BRIEN
Ebb tide in the Docks

The 1960's had passed into history by a mere 20 days . . . yet there could have been no more dramatic illustration of the dawn of a new decade.

On January 20th, 1970, the civic-conscious citizens of Bristol took part in the first City Poll for 23 years – to vote on proposals to close the City Docks to all commercial shipping.

They lent their approval by a clear 5,000 majority to the necessary Parliamentary Bill . . . and the process of converting the Bristol waterfront into what some optimistically predicted would be the New Amsterdam (hadn't New York once been called that!) had begun.

But the old dockland – and its supporters – hadn't given up without a fierce struggle. An up-and-coming young Bristol barrister, Paul Chadd, later to become a Recorder on the Western Circuit, was particularly articulate in defence of the status quo.

The Inland Waterways Association warned that Bristol City Docks would become a 'large municipal duckpond.' Transfer of commercial traffic to Avonmouth would leave the docks barren, it said. And the city council might even be tempted to close the River Avon locks at Cumberland Basin and the Feeder Canal entrance.

How wrong the jeremiad predictions were to prove was signalled just five months later when the majestic iron ship that Bristol gave to 19th century enterprise, the ss Great Britain, came home propelled by 20th century faith and skill.

The incredible 9,000-mile journey from the Falkland Islands – the long-abandoned hulk of Brunel's ocean masterpiece riding on a salvage pontoon – was in retrospect the key event in the regeneration of the City Docks.

From it emerged the new mix of housing, offices, and leisure and pleasure amenities that has offset, at least in part, Bristol's post-war planning nightmare. All this – bitter conflict, eventual triumph – could scarcely have been forecast at the beginning of the 'Sixties.

Then the waterfront was still fulfilling its historical role that had made Bristol one of the great seafaring cities, and led to a maritime tradition reflected in buildings like the Llandoger Trow, the Cabot Tower, and the bonded warehouses.

Two thousand Bristolians were still directly employed as dockers – some 700 of them working mainly in the City Docks – and the reckoning was that a fifth of Bristol's total workforce was engaged in jobs directly related to the port. Tobacco, the wine trade, timber, all still flourished, and much of the raw material arrived at City Docks' quaysides and was stored in warehouses that had not even dreamed of exhibition centres or commercial radio stations.

Bristol may have grown rich on a heady diet of rum, slaves, sugar and tobacco – the staples of transatlantic commerce – elevating it in the 18th century to England's leading city and port outside London. But it was inevitable that the position could not be maintained, as the Industrial Revolution by-passed the South West of England, and West Indian trade receded.

But the 'feel' of a bustling port, trading day-by-day with the Continent, Ireland, even Africa, remained throughout most of the 1960's, before declining into an inevitable seediness that at the finish saw the City Docks – and thus the rate-paying citizens – lose £200,000 a year.

A number of factors, some of them interlocked, accounted for a downfall that spanned a decade – the difficulty of ever-larger ships negotiating the twisting, tortuous six mile River Avon channel from Avonmouth, the transport revolution that saw cargoes being stored in massive container boxes, the national trend towards road transport, and the planners' policy of restricting development of the wharves.

Yet for most of the 'Sixties there were shiploads of Guinness arriving from Dublin (oh the joy of real Liffey Water, black as night, smooth as syrup, compared with the English version brewed under licence); anthracite from South Wales (a cargo that had lent its name to Welsh Back); timber strands from Sweden; sherry from the bodegas of Spain; newsprint from Norway (Bristol still had two evening papers at the start of the 'Sixties); tobacco from America (the very last cargo, 3,600 cases shipped, of all things, in a Yugoslavian vessel, arrived in September, 1969); general goods from the great European ports of Rotterdam and Antwerp.

And then there were the familiar, chugging sand and gravel dredgers, making their daily sorties under the Clifton Suspension Bridge to garner the harvest of the neighbouring Bristol Channel seabed. Ironically perhaps, they were to become the sole survivor of commercial activity into the 'Seventies and 'Eighties, and a symbol of the rise, fall, and rise again of the City Docks.

Their continuing presence was not achieved without a battle – is anything in Bristol? – throughout the 1960's.

First, the design of Bristol's most ambitious post-war road project, the Cumberland Basin bridge scheme, had to take cognizance of the need to let the sandboats in and out, and thus build in the swing system that has been the bane of rush-hour traffic ever since.

The massive essay in concrete, which finally opened on April 14, 1965, had been so long a-coming that Bristolians rather took it for granted. Yet the mile or so of raised roadway, coiled on a site only a few acres in extent, attracted experts from all over the world to inspect the system. Even Texas, that Mohammed Ali among states, sent a polite request for information about the lofty lamps that illuminated the Cumberland Bridge. Apparently, there was nothing as tall in the Biggest State.

Even the names chosen by the city council for the various roads and bridges told something about Bristol's heritage. They included Humphry Davy Way, Faraday Road, McAdam Way, Brunel Way, Plimsoll Bridge and Cabot Way. Every one a famous inventor, builder or explorer; every one with some connection with the very site on which the Cumberland Basin bridge scheme stands. A veritable cradle of history.

The dredgers came into contention again at the end of the decade when Bristol was promoting its Parliamentary Bill to phase out the City Docks, and special clauses had to be inserted to allow bigger ships in at the authorities' 'discretion'. That discretion holds today.

Shipbuilding also remained a picturesque, if declining, waterfront activity in the 'Sixties. The Albion Dockyard of the Charles Hill Company continued to send a variety of vessels – cargo, lightships, pilot tenders – careering down its slipways, to be pulled up by a rattle of mighty chains before they could collide with the Mardyke opposite. Launches were always big social occasions, often with a brass band playing and a swish lunch afterwards, but as the years passed they become less and less frequent.

Eventually, City Docks shipbuilding was to go the way of other commercial activity, only for a latter-day revival, in the shape of up-market sailing craft, to set the Danvils ringing again. Albion was also to make a permanent contribution to revitalisation, when the ss Great Britain returned to the original drydock where she had been launched by Prince Albert exactly 127 years previously.

If the physical and maritime aspects of the City Docks were changing in the 'Sixties, so too was the human face. Dockers remained the dominant, most colourful characters on the waterfront, but their role – and status – was changing.

Those with long memories can still recall the humiliating days when dockers were casual workers, crowding into 'pens' to be allocated work. They could be hired, or left to go hungry, at the whim of the employers. The establishment of the National Dock Labour scheme during the war had set up training programmes and guaranteed everyone fall-back pay even if there was no work, provided they proved attendance. But they still had to go to the pen, or control point, where they were engaged by the various employers.

Then, in 1967, the Devlin Enquiry into the industry resulted in all registered dockers being engaged by licensed employers. They could not be made redundant, so when the amount of cargo handling work declined, many employers were driven towards bankruptcy. Meanwhile, the dockers flexed their new-found muscle in a series of national and local strikes, and the waterfront warehouses became the scene of heated 8 a.m. union meetings, often attended by Avonmouth colleagues as well. More than one local journalist, viewed as a 'tool' of the capitalist press, not to mention the employers, was threatened with a rapid exit in the direction of the murky water.

By the end of the decade, Bristol's dockers faced either redundancy or the six-mile move downstream to Avonmouth. It was little consolation that they were by no means the only victims of closure.

Harvey Elliott ran a dockside cafe, the sort of pull-up-for-dockers where a 'dish of tea' cost sixpence, and a fish dinner 2s. 10d. His customers were rough and ready, warm and friendly, and his tea was said to be the best in Bristol. As the City Docks faced the major sea change at the end of the 'Sixties, Harvey was thinking of going over to businessmen's lunches. The advance army of the Yuppie revolution had put its head over the parapet.

How the sixties looked

A selection
of advertisements
from the pages
of
The Evening Post

Follow THE LEADER!

First off in style – bonded Orlon*
with the scarf look. Assorted
colours. Top right, sizes 12-18.
Centre, sizes 12-16.
Bottom left, sizes 12-24.
All in 'teen sizes 10-16.

£5.10.

C&A

Christmas Shopping at C & A BROADMEAD, BRISTOL— Open daily until 6 p.m.
Friday's 7 p.m.

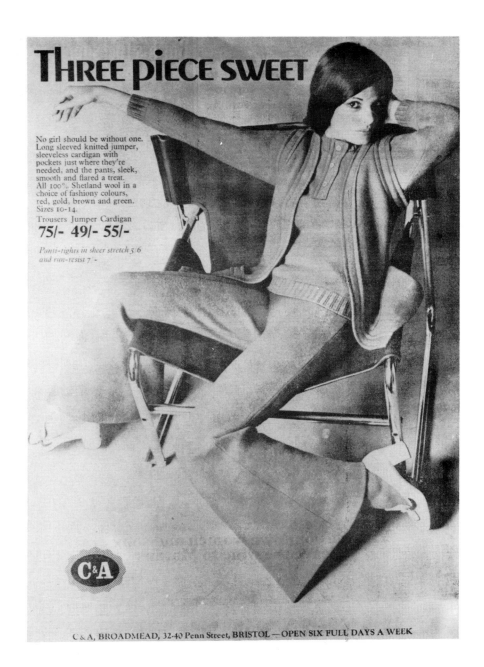

THREE PIECE SWEET

No girl should be without one.
Long sleeved knitted jumper,
sleeveless cardigan with
pockets just where they're
needed, and the pants, sleek,
smooth and flared a treat.
All 100% Shetland wool in a
choice of fashiony colours,
red, gold, brown and green.
Sizes 10-14.

Trousers Jumper Cardigan
75/- 49/- 55/-

*Panti-tights in sheer stretch 5/6
and run-resist 7/-*

C&A

C&A, BROADMEAD, 32-40 Penn Street, BRISTOL — OPEN SIX FULL DAYS A WEEK

NEW
SUNBEAM RAPIER

Built for people who prize individuality...

**Exciting new features plus
rally-bred reliability for those who
always demand the best**

NEW FRONT DISC BRAKES Touch the brake pedal and let the big disc brakes bring you to a safe, sure stop.

POWERFUL NEW ENGINE 'Sports car' acceleration with the new higher compression engine developing 78 b.h.p.

LUXURIOUS NEW INTERIOR With polished wood facia.

STYLISH NEW EXTERIOR Beautiful, sleek lines.

SALOON £695 (plus P.T. £290.14.2) **CONVERTIBLE £735** (plus P.T.£307.7.6)
Whitewall tyres, overdrive on 3rd and 4th gears available as extras

A ROOTES PRODUCT *Call, write or phone for a free trial run today.*
MAIN AGENT :

Telephone:
20031

The *Cathedral Garage* LTD

**COLLEGE GREEN
BRISTOL**

MAKE EATING OUT A PLEASURE IN 1964

Here's a New Year resolution that's fun to make and a joy to keep. And it's as easy as downing a schooner of one of Berni's famous sherries. Explore the nine Berni Inns in Bristol (preferably one at a time) and feel yourself growing more convivial within and decidedly more agreeable without. Make eating out at a Berni Inn a regular date this year. It's a pleasure you'll look forward to!

HORT'S
Broad Street

MOLE IN THE WALL
Queen Square

LLANDOGER TROW
King Street

THE RUMMER
All Saints Lane

THE CROWN
All Saints Lane

THE POSADA
Baldwin Street

THE BRITANNIA
St. Nicholas Street

THE HAWTHORNS
Woodland Rd.,
Clifton

ALL FULLY LICENSED AND OPEN TILL MIDNIGHT

Also Berni's Chicken Barbecue (unlicensed) at The Centre

BOY...
oh, boy...
oh, boy...
oh, boy!

It's part of growing up
when a boy has his first
long trousers–part of
growing up at C & A.

1. All wool worsted suit with
flare line trousers.
Checked in lovat or grey.
Small boys up to 6. £**5.19.**

2. Cotton corduroy
double-breasted navy
jacket. Ages 8-13. £**5.15.**
Fully washable Crimplene*
trousers. In navy, green, fawn,
and checks. Ages 8-13. **75/-**

3. Fully washable Crimplene*
suit. In navy, brown
or blue. Ages 7-13. £**9.19.**

4. Suit in Terylene* and
Sarille*, lined nylon,
is fully washable.
In blue or bronze.
Ages 8-13. £**7.10.**

Grow up at

C&A

*REGISTERED

C&A, BROADMEAD, 32-40 Penn Street, BRISTOL OPEN SIX FULL DAYS A WEEK